Blitz Families

Blitz Families

THE CHILDREN WHO STAYED BEHIND

PENNY STARNS

The
History
Press

For Paul

Front cover photograph: Children playing as air-raid wardens during the Blitz in London. (Mirrorpix); *Back cover photograph*: A West End London Underground air-raid shelter. (NARA/Wikimedia Commons)

First published 2012

The History Press
The Mill, Brimscombe Port
Stroud, Gloucestershire, GL5 2QG
www.thehistorypress.co.uk

© Penny Starns, 2012

The right of Penny Starns to be identified as the Author
of this work has been asserted in accordance with the
Copyrights, Designs and Patents Act 1988.

British Library Cataloguing in Publication Data.
A catalogue record for this book is available from the British Library.

ISBN 978 0 7524 6031 4

Typesetting and origination by The History Press
Printed in Great Britain
Manufacturing managed by Jellyfish Print Solutions Ltd

Contents

Acknowledgements

First and foremost I would like to thank my editor, Sophie Bradshaw, and Abbie Wood and the design, editorial and production staff at The History Press for their excellent work. In addition, there are a great number of people without whom this book would not have been written, and I extend special thanks to Dr Andrew Brindley and his team for all of their help and support. Grateful thanks are due to the Dean, the Very Rev. Dr David Hoyle MA and the Chapter of Bristol Cathedral for allowing the inclusion of pictures of their magnificent memorial windows. I also appreciate the help extended to me by Rachel Brain, Theresa Simeone and residents of Charlton Residential Care for their wartime recollections and pertinent comments. In particular, I thank Rhoda Edmonds and David Gay for giving me so much of their time and attention. The Rev. Canon Brian Arman, his ministerial team, members of the choir and congregation of St Peters Church, Filton, have also been invaluable. Members of the congregation have generously recounted their many memories of Bristol during the Blitz, especially Iris Williams, who prompted a number of thought-provoking discussions about children and war.

My father Edward Starns has contributed enormously to the book by recalling his experiences of the London Blitz and by offering his complete support. Teachers from Birmingham, Coventry, Sheffield, Manchester, Liverpool, Plymouth, Bristol and London have provided me with mounds of evidence gleaned from their own personal experiences of working with city children during the sustained bombing raids of the Second World War. Moreover, survivors from all of these blitzed cities have kindly entrusted me with their childhood stories, which collectively have added a richness and depth to the overall text.

My friends Paul Simeone, Catherine Nile and Jo Denman have provided practical support and encouragement. I am also grateful to my brother Christopher for his previous research assistance, and to my sister Barbara Starns whose co-authored book, *Keeping Children Safe*, provided me with some much-needed context in terms of government child protection policies. I thank my father Edward Starns and my sons James, Michael and Lewis for their love and humour; my grandchildren for their joy and enthusiasm for life; and their mothers for enabling me to share their lives.

Sources

Much of the primary source material for this book rests on the oral history testimonies of individuals who lived through the Blitz. Most of them were children living in cities during the Second World War but others were teachers, paediatricians, social workers or parents. Collectively they have created a remarkable picture of how city children spent their war years. Further information has been obtained from all volumes of the *Journal of Education* (1938–46), *The Times*, Hansard House of Commons and House of Lords Parliamentary Debates for the same period. Primary source material has also been gleaned from Ministry of Health files, Board of Education (Ministry of Education after 1944) documents, and Ministry of Labour records, all of which are held at The National Archives in Kew, London. In addition, numerous files have been consulted in a variety of county record offices across the country.

Secondary sources are listed in the select bibliography at the end of this book. The main secondary works consulted however, are *Children and War* by A. Freud (1943), *The Blitz: The British Under Attack* by J. Gardiner (2010) and *We Are At War: The Diaries of Five Ordinary People in Extraordinary Times* by S. Garfield (2005).

Introduction

Much has been written in recent years about the children who were evacuated during the Second World War under the British government's dispersal policy. Undoubtedly, this civilian evacuation constituted the biggest social upheaval in British history, and in England alone official figures record that 673,000 unaccompanied schoolchildren, 406,000 mothers and young children and 3,000 expectant mothers were moved during the course of three days. In Scotland evacuation figures were estimated as 175,000, of which 50,000 were unaccompanied children. Journalists of the period described the initial evacuation as an exodus of biblical proportions. Subsequent waves of evacuation were more ad hoc in nature but, nonetheless, had profound and long-lasting effects on British society. However, because the historical spotlight has lingered on the children that were evacuated, a larger and more significant group of children have been overlooked. In actual fact, official figures suggest that only 47 per cent of English schoolchildren were evacuated in the initial wave, and only 38 per cent of Scottish school children. The remainder stayed steadfastly in the cities with their parents. Surprisingly, historical literature and analysis of the Second World War period has hitherto and systematically ignored this fact.

Indeed, there were vast numbers of parents who chose to ignore the dire warnings of government ministers before the war and refused to heed the calls for evacuation. Instead, they kept their children with them in cities for the duration of the war. These children endured sustained bombing raids in addition to educational and welfare problems, but new research suggests that the city children who survived the Blitz emerged from the war years emotionally, mentally and physically far healthier than their counterparts who were evacuated to the country. In fact, the ways in which children developed during the war completely baffled government ministers and for the first time in British history local authorities were forced to take on board a whole host of new ideas pertaining to child welfare. Contrary to Ministry of Health expectations, throughout the war years children were growing taller and more robust in the cities than they were in the country areas. This situation did not make sense, either to government ministers or child welfare officers. Country areas were reasonably considered to be healthy environments, with children having access to clean, fresh air and an abundance of healthy fruit and vegetables. The popular image of hearty country children helping to work the land and enjoying the fruits of their labour was also encouraged by government ministers in an effort to underpin official evacuation schemes. But children defied all predictions in terms of child development. Even when nutritional improvements to children's diets were on a par across the length and breadth of Britain, the anomaly remained. The Ministry of Health at one stage concluded that children in the country moved around too much and, therefore, became far too active to grow! They also surmised that city children, by comparison, sat and read comics, thereby reserving their energy for essential growth. All of this was nonsense of course, but it took some time to persuade officials otherwise.

It is also important to recognise that notions of childhood changed dramatically during the war; both in terms of public perceptions and in terms of government policy. At the outbreak of war in 1939 there was a concerted effort to protect children from all mention of war; yet by 1941 children became an integral part of the war effort and nearly every family had been touched by the conflict. Conflicting policies with regard to children became the norm. The Ministry of Labour, for instance, required children to work on the land and in factories as part of the overall war effort, whereas the Board of Education argued that children needed to remain in school and focus on learning. Ministry of Health officials were thus required to tread a delicate policy-making path between the two. In addition to this problem, the latter were also up against local authority opposition for the duration of the war. In the early stages of the war local authorities often ignored the policies which emanated from Whitehall, so very few were implemented. Central government had attempted to offload responsibility for children onto local authorities, but a mixture of obstinacy and lack of resources thwarted this move. By 1941 central government was firmly back in the child policy driving seat. Astonishingly, from this time on, the Ministry of Health managed to push through a number of barriers to reform and introduce significant public health measures. Understandably, the ministers who introduced such policies as improved nutrition, the relocation of many children into the countryside and vaccination programmes, were eager to find evidence of their efficacy. They were particularly keen to find evidence that children were healthier in the country because this would endorse the validity and rationale behind their evacuation policy. The fact that children appeared to be healthier in the cities rather than the countryside defied all explanation.

Eventually, it was a pioneering psychologist named Anna Freud who provided adequate explanations as to why city children, who were dwelling with family members, developed at a quicker rate than evacuees. Anna conducted extensive research into child development and children's relationships throughout the war. In so doing, she proved beyond doubt that the emotional wellbeing of children was essential for their adequate physical and mental growth. Henceforth, there was a proliferation of child guidance clinics across the country and child welfare officers were educated about the emotional needs of the child for the first time. City children, who were virtually raised on bombsites, thus became the key to understanding family relationships and to what extent emotional ties dictated overall child development. By focussing on children who were not evacuated, *Blitz Families* sheds light on the importance of family unity and children's emotional security. The book also reveals some surprising, uplifting and personal accounts of wartime history.

1

Protecting the Nation

O ne of the most pervading myths in British history is the notion that Britain was totally unprepared for the Second World War. Undoubtedly there were economic constraints during the inter-war period as the country struggled to recover from the debts it had incurred as a result of the First World War, and to some extent these constraints naturally underpinned the concerted efforts that were taken by Britain and France to avoid further conflict. Historical evidence also reveals that the appeasement policy pursued by British Conservative Prime Minister Neville Chamberlain towards Hitler in the late 1930s bought Britain some much-needed rearmament time. Aircraft production was increased dramatically from 1934 onwards, and between 1936 and 1939 numerous shadow factories were built. These latter constructions were industrial works that were built with military production in mind, alongside ordinary civilian factories.

During this period twenty-seven new ordnance works were established and, in terms of protecting the nation in readiness for a further war with Germany, British government ministers were far ahead of other European nations – beginning to plan civil defence strategies in 1922. They had realised that the main threat in any future war would come in the form of aerial bombardment, which was later confirmed by the unrelenting air raids experienced by Barcelona during the Spanish Civil War. It was therefore deemed pertinent to discuss the prospect of moving all non-essential persons away from potential danger areas into places of relative safety. Aside from the substantial risk of aerial bombing raids, military personnel pointed out that major cities could become actual fields of combat should an invasion occur, and civilians would impede the fighting forces. Worse still, there was a distinct possibility that they could be taken hostage by the enemy in an attempt to force a British surrender. It seemed sensible then, in the event of war, to remove all non-combatants, particularly vulnerable sections of the population to areas that were not obvious military targets.

There were a few alternatives to an evacuation scheme, and these were debated at length in the House of Commons, but none were considered feasible. A few ministers suggested the erection of specialised camps on the outskirts of major cities, but at this stage it was feared that such camps would look like military bases from the air and would thus become targets for enemy attack. In March 1938, Lord Haldane suggested that deep underground shelters were the way forward. The experience of the Spanish during the Civil War, which began in 1936, indicated that deep shelters were more useful in terms of civil defence and that evacuation was a somewhat flawed policy. Evidently the emotional ties that bound Spanish families together had resisted all attempts at separation and deep shelters were constructed in major cities in order to protect the population from aerial bombardment. Lord Haldane also advised that such shelters could later be used as underground car parks; this potential long-term use would offset the initial building costs.

But it was difficult for British ministers to second guess the enemy during civil defence planning stages. Debates played out in the House of Commons demonstrated considerable support for deep shelters – and nobody doubted the protection that such shelters could provide – but they were also very costly and time-consuming to erect. More importantly, it was thought by some military personnel that deep shelters could potentially become the target of gas attacks if the enemy decided to use chemical warfare. The provision of gas masks for the population and instructions on their use were already included within the overall civil defence strategy as a precaution. Chemical warfare had featured during the First World War and there was a strong possibility that the enemy would deploy chemical weapons again. Thus, while the merits and drawbacks of alternative schemes were highlighted in official circles, evacuation quickly emerged as the only sensible and feasible option for keeping non-combatant personnel safe. Crucially, the policy also received support from senior officers within the armed forces. Colonel Wedgwood, who was an avid protagonist for a civilian evacuation scheme, pointed out that the lack of such a scheme would severely undermine the efforts of fighting men. He argued on a number of occasions that civilian evacuation was essential in terms of maintaining military morale:

> Imagine for one moment that this country is invaded. Every man worth his salt will be engaged either in the field, or in some munitions factory far from his family. All the time they will be desperately anxious about what is happening to their wives, and children and parents ... Therefore, this problem of evacuation is a very real one and does not apply solely to children. It applies to all useless mouths in every country which is meeting this new form of gangster warfare.[1]

In order to devise an efficient and comprehensive civil defence programme a sub-committee of the Imperial Defence Committee was formed in 1932 and the Air Raid Precaution Bill was presented to Parliament in 1937. The Home Secretary subsequently introduced a clause in the bill which effectively called upon all local authorities in England to provide central government with the information it required to prepare a civilian evacuation scheme. The task of co-ordinating all civil defence planning was then given to Sir John Anderson, a senior civil servant with an astounding and excellent reputation for administration and attention to detail.

The Anderson Committee first convened in May 1938 and members began their work by dividing the British landscape into designated evacuation, reception and neutral areas. Senior military personnel from all branches of the armed forces were called upon to advise the committee. These officers duly outlined all military bases, industrial areas and cities that were likely to be attacked. On 28 June 1938 Wing Commander R.V. Goddard also strongly advised Anderson not to evacuate civilians to the east coast, since this stretch of land was nearest to Europe and would, therefore, be the most vulnerable to the threat of bombing and invasion. In addition to constructing and implementing plans for a civilian evacuation scheme, Anderson was also responsible for prioritising essential public services, maintaining public order and safety, controlling transport systems and billeting evacuees. He is best remembered, however, for the protective little tin air-raid shelter that bore his name, and which most people kept at the bottom of their gardens in preparation for the German Luftwaffe raids.

An example of an old Anderson shelter, currently on display outside the Bedford Museum, Bedford.

By 26 July 1938 the Anderson Committee had drafted a final report with regard to civilian evacuation and made several recommendations. Available accommodation in reception areas was to be provided by private householders; it would be compulsory for them to take in evacuees. The government would bear the brunt of evacuation costs but some families would be expected to contribute towards the upkeep of their offspring. In order to maintain industrial production non-essential personnel, such as the sick, would be evacuated in addition to children. It was also decided that civilian evacuation should be a voluntary process. This latter decision subsequently proved to be the most controversial of Anderson's recommendations. Although historical records suggest that British government ministers were reluctant to adopt an overly authoritarian approach towards the issue of evacuation – for fear of being compared with the fascist dictators of Europe – the decision also reflected a genuine ministerial belief in the art of official persuasion.

Nevertheless, a central government policy that originated in Whitehall did not necessarily have widespread support within individual local authorities, many of which lacked the resources and administrative networks that would be required to cope with large numbers of evacuees. From a government standpoint the evacuation scheme was, to some extent, a straightforward exercise in military logistics, but as the social historian Richard Titmuss pointed out:

> The Government were asking a great deal, it was asking parents to send their children for an indefinite period to an unknown destination, there to be committed to the care of strangers. In helping parents make up their minds, much depended, therefore, on the efficiency of local preparations in each evacuation area and particularly on the quality of the relationship between those responsible for the preparatory work – from councillors to teachers – and parents. The art of democratic persuasion, of making people feel confident in the Government's plans, had to be practiced on a local level as well as a national level.[2]

Unfortunately local health and education authorities were none too keen on embracing the official evacuation scheme. They were not included in the government's consultation process and though Anderson had devised an excellent system for transporting evacuees out of the cities, he had not given much thought to how essential services would sustain them in the rural areas. Much of the problem lay with the decision to make the hosting of evacuees compulsory, whilst making the evacuation a voluntary endeavour. As a consequence, a groundswell of resentment surfaced amongst those who would be forced to play host to evacuees against their will, and neither central government nor local authorities could predict the numbers of evacuees who would be involved in the scheme until the process of evacuation began. This situation was clearly a recipe for chaos; one that was not lost on the public as a whole. The problem was further compounded by the fact that evacuee billets were not assessed in terms of the suitability of hosts to look after children, but merely in terms of availability of accommodation. In theory, disabled people and the elderly were exempt from hosting evacuees, but guidelines were often ignored in this respect.

A survey of potential billets for evacuees was initiated by central government in January 1939 and, by this stage, official responsibility for the evacuation

scheme had been transferred from the Home Office to the Ministry of Health
– since the latter was viewed more favourably by the general public. An army
of volunteer interviewers, who were referred to as 'visitors' in official circles,
scoured the country and diligently collected information with regard to over
5 million properties. A deluge of Ministry of Health circulars to local councils
outlined the role of these visitors and the precise information required. They
were not allowed to enter private properties but they were expected to make
extensive notes about each property, its location and its owners. The Minister
of Health addressed the nation on the evening of 6 January 1939, outlining his
proposals and appealing for national co-operation as follows:

> There are many big tasks we want to forward in the coming year. We
> want to press on with housing, with health, to make sure that in the
> schools, in the homes, in the factories, in the shops, in the countryside,
> the possibilities which our times open out for a happier life for all are
> secured. But there are possibilities of an emergency ahead, as well as
> possibilities of peace. One of the biggest problems is, undoubtedly what
> is called evacuation, that is to say many people would leave and many
> people ought to leave crowded or dangerous areas in time of war. Who
> are they to be? Where are they to go?
>
> Well, first, I do not want you to think that the policy is to empty our big
> cities. I mean nothing of the sort. Most people will and should stay where
> they are, carrying on with their ordinary duties; for most of us, in fact,
> are engaged in work of real service to our country. There will however, be
> many who should go to places where they will be relatively safer. Of these
> children must come first. There are many children in Great Britain, eight
> million of them. Many of them of course are in places of relative safety.
> But there are a million of these children in London alone. Without doubt
> there would be, in time of trouble, and even when trouble was feared, a
> widespread rush to get children away from dangerous areas. Unless that is
> organised beforehand there will not only be widespread distress amongst
> families in exposed areas, there will be enormous disorganisation in areas
> into which people might flock. Take shops in these areas for instance they
> would be sold out of supplies in twenty four hours if nothing was done.
> To organise this, it is clear that we have to look for homes for children
> mainly in houses where people already are. Empty houses and camps

will be used as far as possible; but mere numbers make it impossible to rely on these alone. We cannot always rely on summer weather. We may have wintry weather like tonight. In the recent storms many camps where children were, had to be cleared into surrounding houses. What will the method be? Schools will be moved as units with their teachers who will continue with their education. These schoolchildren will need both board and lodging. But when children have their mother or someone else to look after them the householder will be asked to provide lodging only. But it is not only the householder; we have all got a part to play. The local authorities will arrange for reception. The government will provide transport, will put money in the householder's purse, and will see that there is food in the shops at reasonable prices for that purse to buy.

I know that money does not settle everything, so the government and the local authorities are doing their best to make allowances for the thousand and one individual differences. We have to see not only that the houses for instance are suitable for children, but that the children are suitable for the homes. We want this to be a matter of real human relationship and affection, a willing host and a willing guest. The whole nation will have to feel itself as one if such a crisis really comes. And remember, no-one can say 'My house will never be destroyed.' It may be for any of us to ask as well as to give this national hospitality.

Is anything going to be done about it immediately? Yes. That is why I am talking to you tonight. Amongst other things, Mr Colville and I are asking local authorities in England Scotland and Wales to make a survey of housing accommodation by the end of next month. What do we want to know? We want information about the number of rooms and the people already in the house. We want to estimate how many people could be properly accommodated, for we don't want either the guests or the hosts to be over crowded. We also want to know the existing responsibilities of the household, whether, for example, the householder is aged or infirm, out all day, or perhaps himself or her self expecting relatives. Whether a farmer for instance, needs his spare rooms for extra workers; or whether the householder needs extra bedding. Obviously the more information we can get the better it will be for everybody.

So householders will shortly be visited and asked for this information. It will be confidential, collected for this emergency purpose alone, and will be used for no other purpose. I hope therefore, that every householder, whatever his or her personal circumstances, will give all possible help to the visitors. Finally, this work differs from most of our work, the real tasks of which I spoke to you when I began. Here our great hope and prayer about this is that it may never be needed at all. But the foundations of our work must be sound if our life is to be happy; and one of the foundation stones of any nation is that it has thought of danger, faced danger, and decided upon action so that in danger it may be secure.[3]

Government guidelines stipulated that evacuees should not be housed in isolated properties, but when visitors toured the country the pressure to find billets often took precedence over location. Their official guidelines also relied heavily on the 1931 census and definitions of overcrowding as defined within the 1935 Housing Act. Accordingly, the billeting standard was founded on one adult person for each habitable room, children under the age of 10 were considered to be half an adult and under twelve months they did not count at all. On this basis the final survey reports indicated that there was enough habitable space for 6,050,000 people. However, there were gross inaccuracies and glaring mistakes within the pages of these final reports. For instance, they failed to take into account the number of houses that had already been requisitioned by other government departments and the workforce of private companies who were also planning to escape from the cities once war was declared. Some properties were also very close to military bases or installations, which made them likely target areas. Furthermore, according to the 1939 census at least 1,100,000 rooms had been allocated to private evacuees by February of that year. When all these anomalies were corrected the final government survey report indicated that there were enough billets for 4,800,000 people. Even these figures were flawed, since in some areas houses could not accommodate extra people because of water and sewage problems.

Nevertheless, central government had made concerted efforts to gain a comprehensive picture of available accommodation, and successfully devised a workable scheme for evacuating civilians in the event of war. The latter was henceforth referred to as the government's dispersal policy. A public information leaflet was issued by the Lord Privy Seal in July 1939 that stated quite simply: 'The purpose of evacuation is to remove from the crowded and vulnerable centres, if an emergency should arise, those, more particularly children, whose presence cannot be of any assistance.'[4]

Officials at Whitehall had reached a general consensus of opinion that in a country the size of Britain it was impossible to guarantee the total safety of civilians. Ministers were thus very careful to refer to reception areas as areas of 'relative' safety. In essence, the dispersal policy simply meant that less people were likely to be killed or injured in any one city or county because the population was dispersed over a wider geographical area. Newspaper articles and radio broadcasts reinforced this message by stating in no uncertain terms that population dispersal was merely designed to reduce the impact of aerial bombardment; the process of evacuation thus by no means offered complete protection from the enemy.

Individual British families received this message with a mixture of suspicion and doubt. Indeed, contemporary public opinion polls revealed a considerable level of distrust in government policy, but these public misgivings were also combined with an attitude of stoical resilience towards Germany. The Munich Agreement of 1938 had returned the Sudetenland to Hitler's Germany, and British Prime Minister Neville Chamberlain had returned from Munich claiming that he had achieved 'peace for our time'. Consequently, British people heaved an enormous sigh of relief and most believed that war had been averted. Yet five months after the Munich Agreement the German army marched into Czechoslovakia and Britain's appeasement policy was officially dead. As European tension rapidly increased a disconcerted British public reluctantly accepted that war was probably unavoidable. The dramatic failure of appeasement however, had undermined confidence in government policy. There was also a corresponding tidal wave of public support for the Conservative MP Winston Churchill, who had warned unstintingly of the German threat long before it became apparent to others within the corridors of power.

In fairness to British government ministers of all parties, civil defence policies were established long before the outbreak of war. But although these policies were obviously designed to protect the nation from enemy attack and invasion, ministers faced an uphill struggle in terms of persuading the public of their merit. Certain measures, such as blocking out light from their homes after dark, practising gas mask drills and erecting Anderson shelters in their gardens, were adopted with little resistance or complaint. The initial closure of cinemas and curtailment of other public leisure facilities were also met with an air of tolerant resignation. Furthermore, there was no shortage of volunteers for air-raid protection wardens, voluntary aid detachment nurses, firewatchers and the Home Guard. But when it came to persuading the British public to part with their children it was quite a different matter, and official persuasion was simply not up to the task.

In an effort to gain parental support for the evacuation scheme the Anderson Committee decided that children needed to be evacuated with their teachers. Parents needed to be reassured that their children would be safe and teachers were in an ideal position to gain parental trust. Teachers had considerable experience in terms of crowd control and had accompanied their schoolchildren to a variety of state occasions such as the coronation. Sir John Anderson argued that children were more likely to heed the instructions of their teachers in the event of an emergency and he persuaded the National Union of Teachers (NUT) to co-operate with his plans.

Sir Frederick Mander, the general secretary of the NUT, agreed with Anderson that evacuation should be voluntary. He also successfully enlisted the support of his members. However, Sir Percival Sharp of the Association of Education Committees highlighted the confusion that reigned within the local education authorities in designated reception areas. Writing in the *Journal of Education* he outlined the potential problems:

> The children are to be evacuated by schools, their teachers with them. But there is no definite understanding as to the relative financial liabilities of the sending authority as regards the cost of education and as regards other costs. More than one Air Raid Precautions Committee has declared that the safety of children actually attending school is no concern of theirs, and that the Education Committee or education authority should get busy in taking all the necessary steps to ensure the safety of children in school. Local education authorities are entirely without information as to what powers they may properly exercise in this connection. They do not know what classes of expenditure, lying outside the range of expenditure on education, they may properly undertake. They do not know what rates of grant will be paid; they do not even know what classes of expenditure will be recognised for grant purposes. In short, the position is wholly unsatisfactory. It is to be doubted whether the Air

Raid Precautions Committee which seeks to unload its responsibilities as regards school children upon the local education authority will receive a merciful sentence at the bar of public opinion if and when children's lives are sacrificed.[5]

In order to protect national security the Anderson Committee had conducted much of its work in secret. This process naturally hampered communication between Whitehall and the general media, thereby creating a level of public confusion. Local authorities were also, from necessity, kept in the dark. The situation did not bode well when it came to encouraging parental support of evacuation. Neither were Anderson's colleagues in government particularly supportive of his efforts to protect the nation. Many of them argued that all of London's Underground stations needed to be boarded up as soon as war was declared because British civilians would simply take to the Underground and live a subterranean existence for the duration of the war. Others maintained that everyone would simply leave the cities in total panic.

Debates about the merits and drawbacks of the government's dispersal policy were played out in national and local newspapers on a daily basis, but many of the facts of the situation and of the threat that was facing the nation in early 1939 were unknown. Government estimates of the expected level of bombing and the time frame for the declaration of war were pure conjecture. The date and time for the proposed civilian evacuation was unknown. There was even some doubt as to whether or not the railway system could cope with the burden of transporting huge numbers to the myriad of reception areas. Transport officials had stated that they could move 100,000 civilians every hour using the London Underground system, but only under bank holiday conditions.[6] When trying to persuade parents to part with their children it was not even possible for government officials to tell parents where their children would be living. Moreover, unbeknown to parents, when dividing Britain into evacuation, reception and neutral areas Anderson chose to ignore the advice of Wing Commander Goddard. Going against all logic and sound military advice the Anderson Committee had designated the east coast of Britain as a reception area.

There were other controversial decisions. The division of the country appeared to have no rhyme or reason. It was possible, for instance, for a person to walk from one part of Sheffield that was designated an evacuation area to another part of the city that was designated a reception area. To the inhabitants of Sheffield this seemed to be a preposterous situation. The Mayor of Hereford was equally confused when informed that the city was to become both a reception and an evacuation area. Generally however, large cities and towns were designated as evacuation areas and rural areas acted as the reception areas. Anderson had also ruled that some cities would act as neutral areas. In these areas civilians were not eligible to be evacuated under the government dispersal scheme, nor were they allowed to receive any evacuees.

Controversially, Bristol and Plymouth were both designated neutral areas and, not surprisingly, the council members of both cities questioned the wisdom of such a dubious decision. Bristol was a thriving port and centre for aircraft manufacture and Plymouth was a crucial naval base; as such they were both potential targets for enemy bombers. Official documents reveal that the rationale for such a decision rested on one basic and fundamentally flawed assumption. It seems that in his calculations and deliberations Anderson clearly assumed France to be a significant and strong military ally, one that would be able to resist and possibly defeat the German army. It did not occur to him for one moment that France would capitulate quickly and spectacularly under a German onslaught. His overall civil defence strategy, therefore, relied heavily on France as a stalwart ally that would ultimately withstand a German invasion. Thus, Anderson reasoned, he could ignore Wing Commander Goddard and evacuate civilians to the east coast of Britain, since France would, in theory, hold off the threat of a German invasion. Moreover he surmised that from a geographical standpoint, in terms of distance the cities of Bristol and Plymouth would be safely out of reach of German bombers. Although Anderson could not have predicted the rapid fall of France or its subsequent Vichy government, he was nevertheless foolish to rely on his own assumptions and ignore British military advice. Anderson's remit was to protect the nation and provide an overall civil defence strategy that was based on a number of potential variables, and military personnel were better able to predict enemy threats to the nation.

Despite Anderson's flawed assumptions, British civil defence strategy was firmly in place by the summer of 1939, but without public support key civil defence measures could not be implemented. In terms of protecting the nation, the government's dispersal policy represented a vital cornerstone of civil defence, yet even on the brink of war it remained an unpopular and emotive bone of contention for the nation's parents. In essence, the evacuation scheme would stand or fall on the government's ability to persuade parents to part with their children for an indefinite period of time.

Notes

1   Hansard House of Commons Parliamentary Debates, 5th Series, 15 June 1940, col. 1411–1454.

2   Titmuss, R., *The History of the Second World War: Problems of Social Policy* (HMSO, 1950), p. 105.

3   BBC radio broadcast entitled The Transfer of Population in Time of War, by Mr Walter Elliot, Minister of Health, 6 January 1939.

4   'Evacuation Why and How?' public information leaflet no.3, issued by the Lord Privy Seal's Office, July 1939.

5   Sharp, P., 'Week by Week' in *Journal of Education*, vol. IXIII, no. 1881, 27 January 1939, p. 122.

6   For a detailed picture of the railway system planning for evacuation please see Parsons, M., *I'll Take That One* (Peterborough, 1998), pp. 36–42.

2

A Mother's Dilemma

O pinion polls conducted during the late 1930s confirmed that the majority of husbands deferred to their wives when the issue of child evacuation was discussed in homes across the country. Issues of childcare usually fell within mothers' sphere of influence whilst issues of money and work dominated husbands' concerns. In this sense, gender divisions within British society still complied largely with Victorian notions of separate spheres for men and women. Men were expected to find gainful employment to support their families and a legal marriage bar operated in most professional circles, which ensured that women gave up all notions of a career once they were married. Housewives devoted their time towards caring for husbands and children within a very traditional family framework. Older members of the family often lived nearby and very few people ventured further than their own immediate local area for work or leisure activities. Working-class families were particularly close knit and the prospect of sending children away to strange, potentially hostile environments for any length of time was a scenario that shook the very foundations of family life.

According to Gallup opinion polls only 42 per cent of parents were in favour of compulsory evacuation, compared to 50 per cent who preferred the voluntary option. Only 8 per cent were undecided about the issue and stated that they needed more information before they could reach any conclusion. When asked if they were in favour of private billeting parents were less hesitant, most claiming that they would prefer children to be housed in specially constructed camps supervised by teachers. The option of private billets was preferred by 25 per cent, whereas 72 per cent favoured the notion of housing children in camps; only 3 per cent were undecided.[1]

Thus it was clear that the government dispersal scheme, based as it was on a system of private billeting, did not have widespread public support. Neither could it be argued that government ministers – even with the best will in the world – had mastered the art of persuading parents, and mothers in particular, of the merits of dispersal. They lacked the emotional empathy that was required to connect with anxious mothers, many of whom sat by their firesides night after night while their children were tucked up in bed, listening to the depressing news of looming war. Prior to the Second World War female government ministers were few and far between and it was difficult to ascertain a woman's ministerial view with regard to evacuation. Dr Edith Summerskill MP was a voice crying in the wilderness when she expressed sympathy for the mothers' dilemma in the House of Commons and highlighted the emotional dimension of dispersal. Protesting in Whitehall after a series of BBC radio broadcasts were issued by the Minister of Health, Summerskill pointed out that:

A stereotyped speech from a Minister does not reach a woman who is going to part with her children. I sat there [listening to a radio appeal] receptive to the Minister, but he did not move me emotionally one iota, and that is not because I know him so well. He gave the speech of a Statesman, just as the Chancellor of the Exchequer might be speaking to the nation and saying 'now I am going to put an extra tax on you.' The Minister was speaking to women who are in turmoil of emotion, to women saying to themselves, 'the only thing in life that matters to me are my children running around me. They have my face, my hair my eyes.' And the Minister comes on and says in a statesmanlike way, 'You are to be evacuated. The teachers are ready. Get things packed. It is the right thing to do.' And then he goes on to say that it is a question of dispersal, that if a bomb drops on a place in the country it will not kill as many people as if it drops on a crowded town. Why do those women worry about that? They want you to come to them tenderly and compassionately. Some of these mothers are thinking 'Freddie has only got one decent pair of trousers. How can I send him away to strangers?'[2]

This statement was received with a degree of astonishment and bewilderment in the House of Commons. Planning for evacuation had countenanced logistical problems, but it was fair to say that emotional considerations had not entered into the process of policy formulation in the slightest. When committee members had sat around large polished tables shuffling their pieces of paper, quoting statistics and discussing transport arrangements, no one had even mentioned the possible emotional and psychological impact of evacuation. Until the latter stages of Anderson's deliberations the committee was dominated by men. Two women were eventually added to the committee when a male civil servant pointed out half the evacuees would be young girls, and that perhaps a little female advice might be useful! In fact, Anderson was described by many of his contemporaries as follows:

> He was civil servant par excellence, but devoid of any emotion.
>
> He was not friendly in any way he had no sense of humour as far as I know, no sense of the aesthetic. If I say Anderson was inhuman I am risk of being misunderstood but he didn't have the normal sentiments. He was a great administrator and he had a lot of background, he was a man that you turned to naturally.[3]

Much of the problem however, stemmed from the fact that most politicians and senior civil servants at this time came from upper-class backgrounds, as such, they were accustomed to leaving home at the age of 7 to attend public boarding schools. Thus Anderson Committee members found it difficult to identify with other sections of society where this process was not the norm. It was amid guffaws and cries of derision from male ministers of all political parties that Summerskill continued to drive home her point:

> The Minister opened his statement by discussing compulsory powers. Many people have come to me in the House and asked 'are you for or against compulsion?' The Committee seems to be rather divided on the point. I hope the Minister will not adopt such drastic measures too early for this reason, that in the problem of evacuation the greatest difficulty with which he is faced is not accommodation in the reception areas, is not transport, is not schooling, but the fact that parents will not allow their children to go away. He says 'I have the trains, the local authorities are

waiting to take the children, the schools are ready for them, but I cannot get the parents to say yes.' I want to tell him, though I am sure he will not agree with me, why there has been this lack of response. What is it he is asking these parents to do? When I say parents it really means mothers, because it is generally the mother who has the last word. He is not asking them to pay a tax, he is not even asking them to pay an excess profits tax, or join the A.R.P. or give up their time for war work; he is asking them to suppress the strongest instinct in any human being, and part with their children. I feel that the government have not realized the fundamental psychological problem which confronts them. Let me remind the Minister of the life of a working class house wife. Her life has been one of drudgery from the time she got married, and when she thinks upon her life her only compensation, the only thing that makes her say 'well it has been worthwhile,' is for her to look at her children. She has created them; she has fed them. In all those homes her life revolves around her children. Surely, then, the Minister should ask himself what is the best way to reach a mother.[4]

Summerskill was correct in her assumption that emotional considerations had been overlooked during the planning stages for population dispersal. It was also possible that class distinctions had influenced a lack of official empathy with the working class. However it would be wrong to assume that working-class parents were any more or less emotionally attached to their children than parents in other sections of British society. Traditionally, although upper-class parents sent their children away from the family home to boarding schools at an early age, they did so in the safe and certain knowledge that these schools possessed excellent reputations, and were well vetted and monitored. It is highly likely that these same upper-class parents would not be quite so eager to send their children to live in unknown environments with total strangers.

Similarly, middle- and working-class parents were not averse to sending their children to live in specially constructed school camps if they could be supervised by professional teachers, as the opinion polls had confirmed. Indeed, parents generally were not so overwhelmed by tidal waves of emotion as to neglect basic common sense. Moreover, evidence suggests that parents understood government arguments and logic behind the dispersal policy perfectly. The majority of them however, were understandably reluctant to subject their offspring to a lottery in terms of living accommodation and host parents. Certainly emotions played a part in the decision-making process, but it seems that most parents were prepared to endure the emotional wrench of parting with their children if they could be sure of their safety in reception areas. The system of private billeting did not offer this surety.

During the summer of 1939 parents voiced numerous concerns about potential billeting standards in reception areas, the suitability of host families and the long-term schooling, health and welfare of their children. Questions were submitted to local councils and government offices, such as how often could parents visit their children? Would they be able to return home for Christmas or family celebrations? Would their children have to work on farms or be involved in other forms of war work? Was it likely for children in reception areas to be able to attend church services of their own religious faith? Would parents be informed if their offspring were ill or severely homesick? How would child welfare be monitored? All reasonable questions that demanded answers if parents were to be adequately reassured. But other than to state that host parents in reception areas would assume parental responsibilities in all matters pertaining to child evacuee welfare, official advice was limited. Government ministers appeared to believe that all adults would act in a responsible and protective manner towards evacuee children. It is reasonable to suggest, however, that individual parents did not readily share this belief. In an era when extended family networks were the norm, discussions about evacuation tended to involve grandparents, uncles, aunts, siblings and cousins. Furthermore, an air of tension and tangible nervousness descended on families across Britain as the build up to war intensified. Adults took great care to shield the children from any talk of war but children noted the dramatic change in atmosphere. Two young girls from separate families recalled their impressions thus: 'There was a feeling of great fear in the air. All the adults were very cross and talked about things and used to go "sshhh" when we children came into the room.'[5] 'There was always a feeling that there was going to be trouble. That was always present even though we were young.'[6]

When all things were considered, a mother living in an evacuation area had a basic dilemma. Was it better to keep her children with her and face the German bombers together? Or was it more sensible to entrust her children to the care of strangers who were living in reception areas? Much depended on the character of individual mothers, their children and the degree of family support. Mothers with children of a nervous disposition, for instance, were more likely to keep their children close – as did those whose children were sick or disabled. On the other hand, there were some mothers who viewed the dispersal policy as an opportunity to be free of domestic ties and child-rearing responsibilities, though these were few and far between. Most mothers were racked with angst at the thought of parting with their children and the decision to keep them at home was often made at the last minute.

Doubts about the potential effectiveness of the government scheme and financial considerations dictated some family decisions. Host families in reception areas were to be paid 10 shillings and sixpence for the first unaccompanied child they housed, and 8 shillings and sixpence for any subsequent children. Arrangements were made for hosts to collect weekly payments in advance at local post offices. Initially this money would be paid by the government, but eventually parents of evacuated children would be expected to contribute to this allowance. Many working-class parents were not in a position to pay towards the upkeep of children in reception areas, particularly those with large families. It was proposed under the government scheme that mothers could accompany very young children into the reception areas and these women would pay a sum of 5 shillings to host families for their own upkeep and 3 shillings for their child. These mothers could claim payments from the Ministry of Labour Office. In these pre-NHS days, if an evacuee was ill or required medical attention then local authorities would be expected to foot the bill. In theory, central government appeared to have thought through many of the financial implications of evacuation, but in practice the failure to consult local authorities about some policy decisions backfired dramatically. Subsequently ludicrous situations arose, whereby many pregnant women who were evacuated from cities were shunted from one reception area to another and back again, because no local authority wanted to pick up the bill for their medical care and confinements.

However, there is evidence that government ministers had taken on board parental concerns about the issue of private billeting. The National Camps Corporation was established in 1938 with a view to providing supplementary accommodation for children once war broke out. The president of the Board of Education, Lord De La Warr, provided the impetus for the Camps Act of May 1939. This legislation placed the camps at the disposal of the Ministry of Health and the Board of Education. After a considerable amount of wrangling between various government departments thirty-two sites were chosen for the erection of purpose-built camps. These were situated on the fringes of large cities. Fifteen camps were proposed for the perimeter of London, three for Birmingham, six for Manchester and Liverpool, three for Leeds and Bradford, two for Newcastle, and one each for Sheffield, Hull and Portsmouth. But even before the camp schools were built the Board of Education and the Ministry of Health were inundated with requests from other interested parties requiring accommodation. Most of these requests came from the Air Ministry and industrial establishments, all of whom desperately needed housing for their recruits and workforce. Lord De La Warr, who had personally donated some of his own land in Ashdown Forest for one of the campsites, insisted that all camps should be used by schoolchildren. Nevertheless, from a parental standpoint, camp schools had no bearing on their decision whether or not to comply with the government's dispersal policy, since none of the camps were completed before war was declared. The MP Mr Hicks apologised for this state of affairs, claiming that:

> We lost more than one site because of the objections that were put forward, many of them frivolous. Delay occurred between the times when objections were raised, and when we were able to approve a site, but this is our democratic system of going around and giving everyone a chance of sticking their nose in.[7]

While government officials wrangled with the issue of camp schools, preparations were being made elsewhere to soften the potential blow of parent–child separation. Amongst these preparations a special song was written for children by Gaby Rogers and Harry Philips entitled *Goodnight Children Everywhere*. This song, written in 1939, was originally broadcast by none other than Gracie Fields and it became an important childrens' wartime anthem. With poignant, tender words and music the song literally did reach out to children everywhere, and every evening courtesy of the British Broadcasting Corporation (BBC):

> Sleepy little eyes in a sleepy little head,
> Sleepy time is drawing near.
> In a little while you'll be tucked up in your bed,
> Here's a song for baby dear.

Goodnight children everywhere,
Your mummy thinks of you tonight.
Lay your head upon your pillow,
Don't be a kid or a weeping willow.
Close your eyes and say a prayer,
And surely you can find a kiss to spare.
Though you are far away, she's with you night and day,
Goodnight children everywhere.

Soon the moon will rise, and caress you with its beams,
While the shadows softly creep.
With a happy smile you will be wrapped up in your dreams,
Baby will be fast asleep. Goodnight children everywhere.[8]

Yet no amount of sentimental songs and softly, softly persuasion tactics were going to convince more resolute mothers to part with their children. Confronted by a government dispersal policy that contained many unknown variables, and facing the prospect of subjecting their children to the random fortunes of private billeting, it was perhaps not surprising that over 50 per cent of English and Scottish mothers chose to keep their children with them in the cities rather than comply with dispersal. These mothers initially adopted a 'let's wait and see' approach to the advent of war; many of them later deciding to weather the air raids and deprivations of war together as a family unit rather than separate. When the British government issued the order to 'evacuate forthwith' on 31 August 1939, therefore, the numbers of evacuees fell considerably short of government expectations. Over a period of three days 1,500,000 British children were moved from cities to rural areas, but this figure amounted to only 47 per cent of all English schoolchildren and 38 per cent of Scottish schoolchildren. Newspaper journalists described the evacuation as an exodus of biblical proportions with official figures for England recording the evacuation of 673,000 unaccompanied schoolchildren, 406,000 mothers with young children and 3,000 expectant mothers. Figures for Scotland estimated that 175,000 persons were evacuated, of which 50,000 were unaccompanied children.[9] Lord Allen, who was a junior civil servant at Whitehall at the time, recalled, 'My contemporary impression was that it had gone as well as could be expected'.[10]

Following meticulous planning meetings and numerous public appeals, government ministers were disappointed and frustrated by the low evacuee turnout. Many did find some consolation in the fact that at least transport arrangements had gone smoothly, while some claimed that over-emotional mothers were probably responsible for the lower than expected evacuee figures. Though for some mothers the mere thought of air raids was enough to give them the jitters, as a mother of a young baby confided to her diary:

> I've been very nervy these last two nights, having waking dreams and a recurrence of my old nightmare of the ceiling falling down on top of me. Nowadays, with the possibility of air raids, it has gained in realism and the other night it seemed as if it had really happened at last. The beams of the roof were pressing down upon me, and there was an added terror in water trickling down too. Then I woke and the beams of wood melted away into darkness. The sound of trickling water was explained by the fact that I was clutching the hot water bottle agitatedly. I found the electric light switch and when I put the light on found that in my attempt to get out of bed in a panic I had put one foot into the baby's cot which I had drawn alongside my own bed. She has now been removed to the foot of the bed for safety.[11]

Yet opinion polls, letters to newspaper editors, council and government officials and school log books record decisively that mothers would have given wholehearted support to an evacuation scheme which favoured the housing of their children within specially constructed school camps, particularly if these camps contained teachers that were already known to their children. Undoubtedly some mothers did allow their emotions to dictate their decisions, but it was not self-indulgent maternal emotions that accounted for low evacuee figures, it was the government's decision to rely on a system of private billeting for evacuees. This system amounted to a lottery in terms of providing adequate homes for evacuees. It can reasonably be argued, therefore, that full and unequivocal support of dispersal would have only been forthcoming if school camps had been built in rural areas, in adequate numbers, before the outbreak of war on 3 September 1939.

Notes

1 Gallup, G., *Gallup Opinion Polls: Opinion Polls in Great Britain 1937–1975* (New York University Press, 1976).

2 Hansard House of Commons Parliamentary Debates, 5th Series, 15 June 1940, col. 411–454.

3 Lord Allen BBC interview for Radio 4 programme, *Evacuation: The True Story*, 1999.

4 Hansard House of Commons Parliamentary Debates, 5th Series, 15 June 1940, col. 411–454.

5 Jean Lord BBC interview for Radio 4 programme, *Evacuation: The True Story*, 1999.

6 Elizabeth Paak, ibid.

7 Hansard House of Commons Parliamentary Debates, 5th Series, 12 November 1940, col. 1839.

8 Rogers, G. and Phillips, Harry, *Goodnight Children Everywhere* (1939), first broadcast by Gracie Fields from France with a dedicated 'tender thought to all evacuated children'.

9 Hansard House of Commons Parliamentary Debates, 5th Series, 14 September 1939, col. 824–884.

10 Lord Allen interviewed for the BBC Radio 4 programme, *Evacuation: The True Story*, 1999.

11 Garfield, S., *We Are At War: The Diaries of Five Ordinary People in Extraordinary Times* (2005), p. 174.

3

A New Generation of Artful Dodgers?

*D*uring the three days prior to the outbreak of war on 3 September 1939, 1,500,000 children were evacuated from British cities to areas of relative safety in the surrounding countryside. When women, the disabled and hospital inpatients were included in evacuation figures the total exceeded 3.5 million persons. As a result of this laborious evacuation, some city streets fell eerily silent. The majority of working-class children were used to playing in their neighbourhood streets, and over a thousand different children's street games had been noted at this time.[1] From skipping games and their associated rhymes, to marbles, hopscotch, tag and kicking the can, children were accustomed to amusing themselves noisily amongst the city streets.

It was no surprise, therefore, that adults in some city areas missed the joyful laughter and playful voices of the young. For those children who had remained behind however, lifestyles required a period of considerable readjustment. This was particularly true for children of school age. Since teachers had accompanied evacuees to the reception areas, schools in evacuation areas had closed. The Board of Education wanted to send a clear message to parents in terms of child safety and overall civil defence. Thus members of the board had decided emphatically that it was impossible to guarantee the safety of schoolchildren in evacuation areas and to keep schools open in such areas would constitute an enormous risk. To do so would also send out conflicting messages to parents.

With the closure of schools came other problems in terms of child welfare. Extended and adequately supported families fared reasonably well, but others suffered from neglect. The Ministry of Labour wanted as many women as possible to work in the munitions factories. Indeed, this was envisaged by some ministers as a positive by-product of evacuation. Since by relieving mothers of their maternal duties they would be free to enter the workforce and contribute to the industrial war effort in greater numbers.

Wartime nurseries were established in evacuation areas to accommodate very young children, but those of school age were not catered for in any sense. Some were able to spend time with older family members such as grandparents, while others were left to aimlessly roam the city streets. The majority of city children, however, occupied their time by helping adults in family businesses, such as bakeries or grocery shops. Girls tended to help more with domestic chores, whilst boys were usually asked to run errands for other family members and generally help out with heavier work such as gardening and rubbish collecting. But there were also those who got up to mischief. The majority of men had enlisted in the armed forces and boys undoubtedly mourned the loss of a male role model. This absence of a father figure combined with the lack of schooling and compulsory blackout conditions prompted a certain percentage to enter into a world of crime. In response to this worrying trend, police chiefs in major cities introduced a rigid curfew system for children. Whilst somewhat alarmist, reports in the national press claimed that Britain was breeding a new generation of Artful Dodgers!

In fact, there was no evidence to support the view that British youngsters were embarking on organised crime on a grand scale, and even less to support the notion of a return to Dickensian times – when Fagin type characters exploited homeless juveniles by turning them into pickpockets for their own profit. Indeed, in 1939 the general public were in more danger of being conned by black market racketeers and corrupt adult thieves (who became known as spivs) than they were of suffering at the hands of children, since juvenile crime figures for this year remained reasonably static. But with the closure of schools in evacuation areas there was always a fear that dire wartime circumstances and a lack of parental supervision could possibly encourage more youngsters to stray from the straight and narrow. Writing in the national *Journal of Education* in November 1939 the president of the Board of Education stated:

> We cannot afford as a nation to let three quarters of a million grow up as little barbarians, and the government have not the slightest intention of doing so. There are already some minor activities going on in the schools in the towns – admittedly inadequate on any long terms basis, but nevertheless something. We feel moreover, that, the children in evacuation areas are getting the worst of both worlds. On the one hand they are running a quite unnecessary risk – and on the other they are missing all social care and schooling, and a great number of them are acquiring habits of idleness, if not worse.[2]

The Board of Education was in a very difficult position. Its members could not be seen to endorse the reopening of city schools because this would send out a potentially disastrous message to parents and encourage them to bring children back to the cities. As it was, the board was already facing a losing battle. For the first few months of the war Hitler was preoccupied with eastern Europe and, with the exception of some naval skirmishes off the east coast, there was very little action directed at Britain. This period became known as the 'phoney war' and seemed to vindicate the decision of those mothers who had chosen to keep their offspring with them in the cities. Consequently, this lack of aerial bombardment combined with billeting chaos in the reception areas prompted many returnees. To the government's dismay, by Christmas 1939 it was estimated that over 90 per cent of evacuees had returned to their original city homes. For the Board of Education this was a nightmare scenario. City schools had been closed on 1 September and most were commandeered for civil defence purposes and training within weeks of the closures.

Following some heated discussions at Whitehall, government ministers assembled an urgent conference on 22 January 1940 to re-evaluate their dispersal policy. The Minister for Health and the Home Secretary confirmed the official commitment to dispersal but the latter acknowledged that, 'In some respects the scheme had not fulfilled expectations.'[3]

He continued by stating that the numbers who had taken advantage of the scheme were very disappointing and teething problems had occurred in reception areas, but preparations for further evacuations were entirely necessary.

A New Generation of Artful Dodgers?

The conference members concluded that a two-pronged approach was desirable. City parents who had not yet sent their children to safer areas should be encouraged by all means possible to do so, and those who had sent their children to reception areas should be encouraged to leave them with their host families. Interestingly, the conference minutes reveal that ministers desperately wanted to achieve the collaboration of parents for future evacuations but were at a total loss as to how this could be accomplished. Moreover, none appeared to think in terms of how family ties could be maintained between city parents and their evacuated offspring. They did conclude, however, that the public would not respond to new calls for evacuation at a predetermined date.

New evacuation plans, therefore, needed to be flexible and able to be implemented at a moment's notice, in response to an imminent attack. The Home Secretary also recognised that, 'There must be further arrangements for education. While the position in reception and neutral areas was not unsatisfactory, the position in evacuation areas was far from satisfactory, and every effort would have to be made to release school buildings which had been diverted to civil defence purposes.'[4]

In the event, prompted by a fear of Artful Dodgers, some schools were partially reopened in London's East Ham before Christmas 1939. Nevertheless, in April 1940 over 183,000 children were receiving no education at all and 13,000 were receiving less than half-time instruction.[5] Government policy appeared to be contradictory, however, and ministers had effectively reached an impasse. To argue for the release of school buildings and a reopening of schools in evacuation areas clearly went against the principles of the dispersal policy. Critics of the evacuation conference also argued that important issues of emotional human relationships, child poverty and class distinctions had been studiously overlooked. Neither had anyone considered the vast cultural differences that existed between city and rural communities. Even the Archbishop of Canterbury was moved to voice his concerns with regard to the potential social dislocation of dispersal:

> He [the Archbishop] could foresee a great slackening of the sense of parental responsibility and of the unity of family life. It was quite certain that the matter required far greater and more systematic thought than had yet been given to it, and he hoped that that thought would be given to it before it was too late.[6]

As the prospect of fragmented family life became a reality for many, other clergy members spoke out against the folly of ignoring the importance of emotional ties. Notions of childhood were also in dispute. In 1939 the majority of children usually left school at the age of 14 to seek employment. Defence regulations numbers twenty-nine and thirty of this year also allowed for children aged 13 to be exempt from lessons to help with the war effort, particularly food production. It was estimated in Durham, for example, that 59 per cent of the county's potato crop was picked by schoolchildren.[7] But on leaving school not all 14-year-olds were adept at finding useful employment, and the age of conscription into the armed services was set at 18 years. Local authority statistics suggested that it was during the four years between the ages of 14 and 18 that children were most likely to be enticed into crime, especially if they were growing up without adequate parental guidance and authority.

Artful Dodgers, such as they existed, tended to be male and opportunistic in nature, and fell in the risk category already identified by area police chiefs. Children did not officially become adults until they were aged 21, and police constables consistently pointed out that children left to their own devices would undoubtedly get up to mischief. Moreover, chief constables in provincial areas argued that the situation could be greatly helped by raising the school-leaving age to 16. While juvenile crime figures for 1939 remained static there was a steady and systematic rise in reported juvenile crimes during the following two years, as opportunist thieves stole money and food from bombed-out buildings. But rising juvenile crime was not restricted to evacuation areas. Figures revealed that the social dislocation caused by dispersal had prompted a wave of what police referred to as attention-seeking crime.

As numerous debates surrounded the government dispersal policy, other fundamental concerns also surfaced around this time and became a strong feature of public discourse. These worries were entirely focussed on the attributes of the average British personality. There was apparently some official concern as to whether or not the general public would be able to withstand prolonged bombing raids and mass destruction. Psychiatrist Dr Henry Wilson claimed that some individuals would not be capable of taking care of their own needs once the conflict began in earnest, let alone those of their children. In a public address he claimed:

The problem of wartime nerves is the individual's problem of reaction. Is he going to isolate himself from others and act in a childlike way, dependent, crying out for help to other people, asking others to make the decisions, complaining of this or that, or is he going to allow his own feelings to be merged into those of the group of which he forms a body? In other words, is he going to be a self isolator or a self liquidator? Is he going to recognise responsibility to himself alone, like the persons with panic who forget about their family, or is he to say, in the acute danger through which I am living, here is an opportunity of helping others and helping the community in which I live?[8]

Unbeknown to Dr Wilson and others of a similar ilk, he had partially summed up, in the last few words of his lecture, what eventually became known as the spirit of the Blitz. Since the desire of the British people to pull together in order to defeat a common enemy totally outweighed personal and selfish concerns in all geographical areas and in nearly all circumstances. With the exception of the usual handful of crooks and black market scoundrels Dr Wilson's average British personality far exceeded all professional and official expectations. Furthermore, it was about to be put to the test. In April 1940 Britain was defeated in its Norwegian campaign, and Neville Chamberlain resigned as prime minister. Winston Churchill took over, and the following month German forces invaded Holland. By the end of June, Belgium, the Netherlands and France were occupied by German forces. The phoney war was over and the Blitz began. From September 1940 to May 1941 the German Luftwaffe subjected major British cities and ports to unremitting waves of aerial bombardment. More than 50 per cent of all the civilian casualties of the war – over 80,000 – were sustained during this period. It was some testimony to the British personality, therefore, when a Gallop opinion poll conducted at this devastating time recorded that people were more depressed by the British weather than by Hitler's bombs. Dame Katherine Raven was a nurse on duty at St Bartholomew's (Barts) Hospital and described the first night of the London Blitz and subsequent air raids as follows:

In August a few bombs were dropped on the city, but it was not until September the 7th that we experienced the whole fury and might of the enemy. At 5 p.m. I remember it was still daylight, waves of German bombers dropped their bombs on the city and the docks and the East End. Casualties were coming in, the whole sky was like a great red sunset in the wrong place – in the east – and this immense vivid red light guided the next onslaught which came at 7 p.m. Barts was hit that night. I was caring for casualties on the first floor of the new block when I was blown right across the ward, the blast taking the window and all before it. I was unhurt. Hundreds of casualties were brought to us that night, the theatres worked non stop and the doctors and nurses worked together day and night. We patched up the charred and broken bodies and as soon as they were fit to move we saw them off to Hill End on the Green Line ambulances – to prepare beds for the next onslaught. By this time the underground stations were being used as air raid shelters, and every evening henceforth, if one happened to venture outside, one could witness queues of people with some bedding waiting to buy a 1.1/2d ticket for the tube where they spent the night. As the war proceeded, chalk or paint marks were made on the platforms allotting space to the families and the electricity on the tubes was cut, so that more people could shelter underground on the actual rails and in tunnels and even on the stationary escalators. It was a sight never to be forgotten. I think one of the worst nights for us, as regards pain and sorrow and death, was when bombs blasted through the Bank underground stations, carrying the flaming debris right down to the platforms and burying the people taking refuge there, and burning them so as to be unrecognisable. Many, many casualties were brought to us that night and I have never seen such burns in my life – black charred bodies, still alive. We had to do our best. Nurses performed things in 1940 that were unheard of previously.[9]

Although Hitler's aim was to beat the British people into submission, the continual aerial bombardment actually had the opposite effect and succeeded in galvanising the population into brave, defiant and determined defenders of their homeland. The British people and their war effort became a force to be reckoned with and, perhaps surprisingly, children played a hitherto unacknowledged but crucial role within the overall endeavour to achieve victory. Children as young as 5 could be found working in rural areas on farms and in dairies, whereas those in the city worked in factories, shops and offices. They also helped to maintain morale. What had been termed as the 'problem'

Firefighters at work in a bomb-damaged street in London, after a Saturday night raid, c. 1941. (*New York Times* Paris Bureau Collection/Wikimedia Commons)

age group quickly became absorbed into flourishing cadet schemes that were organised by civilian and military administrations alike. Girls, for instance, were able to join cadet nursing schemes that were established to ease the labour shortages of the civil nursing reserve at the age of 15. And boys of 14 and upwards were incorporated into army, navy and air force cadet schemes. These measures did not entirely halt the rise in juvenile crime – there were increasing opportunities for thieves to indulge in the looting of homes already damaged by bombs as the war progressed – but the need to confront the devastation caused by the Blitz undoubtedly shifted personal priorities, and possessions did not seem nearly as important when faced with enormous casualty rates and loss of life. Subsequently, there was less focus on the issue of Artful Dodgers and a growing recognition that most young teenagers were becoming an essential component of both the emergency services and the armed forces.

In response to the Blitz, government agencies quickly stepped into action to organise a new exodus from designated evacuation areas. On this occasion people were generally more amenable to leaving their homes since bombing raids were already destroying the very fabric of the neighbourhoods around them. Country hosts were also more agreeable and sympathetic towards their city counterparts than they had been in 1939. When news of the Blitz reached rural areas most people responded quickly by rallying around to help the incoming city folk, many of whom were scared, exhausted and homeless. But despite the unremitting onslaught of hell and fury targeted on cities by the Luftwaffe, there remained stalwart families who refused to leave the cities and refused to be separated. Consequently, there were renewed calls for evacuation to be made compulsory. *The Times* newspaper became a leading protagonist for such a policy. In its leading article of 18 November 1940 it outlined the issue as succinctly and forcefully as possible:

> The core of the trouble is the number of people still in London who cannot be described as necessary residents – necessary to its industry and to the care of those who have to stay. This has led to congestion in shelters never planned as dormitories, and to the creation of undesirable conditions in many of them. More unnecessary residents have therefore to be sent away and comfortable and sanitary conditions created for the residue of necessary residents. The question is whether this can be done as long as evacuation remains voluntary and so long as no central authority exists both to devise and operate shelter policy. Much has been done, but 279,000 schoolchildren out of a total of 842,000 before the war are still in the London evacuation areas, in addition to tens of thousands of persons who can also be spared and should be moved. By all means let the resources of persuasion – already extensively drawn upon – and must be used to the full. The arguments against compulsion are many

and strong. But in the last resort nothing can override the necessity for disencumbering a great city of those who involuntarily impede its war effort and for preventing vast numbers of children from running wild.[10]

In addition to the school-aged children and teenagers who remained in London and other major cities, from 1940 onwards were another vulnerable group, the under-5s. Accurate figures of these children are difficult to attain however, because some were travelling back and forth with family members between city and country areas throughout the war, and numerous records were lost as a result of bombing raids. The city's child population was also rising at an alarming rate between 1940 and 1941, with babies often being born in Underground stations and air-raid shelters. Despite renewed calls for compulsory evacuation, almost a third of all mothers in evacuation areas decided to ride out the storm and keep their children with them. Rationales for this decision varied, but most had reasoned that with their husbands away fighting in the armed forces with no guarantee of their return, there was a distinct possibility of their children becoming orphans if they, as mothers, remained in the cities but sent their children away to the country. This fear was associated not only with the potential consequences of aerial bombardment, but also of a German invasion. City mothers explained that the prospect of dying together as a family unit was infinitely preferable to the separation of family ties. It is likely that returning evacuees also influenced their decision, since many told stories of hostile host families and chaos in reception areas. Prevailing attitudes also reveal that in many respects the refusal of mothers to part with their children was inextricably linked with the defiant spirit of the Blitz.

Children epitomised the future, a time when Britain would be victorious and families could all look forward to a happier and more secure post-war world. National press agencies continued to publish alarmist reports about children becoming Artful Dodgers and consistently outlined the difficulties and risks of keeping children in cities. Additionally, such articles often criticised mothers for being stubborn and defiant. Yet it can also be argued that this same stubbornness and defiance was inherent within the British people, the manifestations of which became famously renowned as a bulldog spirit. Indeed, they were the very characteristics which provided the foundations of wartime morale. Moreover, regardless of the press clamours for compulsion with regard to evacuation, members of the British government were determined to operate as a caring democracy rather than a totalitarian state. It is to their credit, therefore, that civilian evacuation remained a choice for individuals throughout the war, rather than an enforced command.

Juvenile crime did continue to rise in all major cities during the Blitz however, as the chief constable for Manchester police force reported in 1941: 'There has, with the exception of 1939, been a steady and systematic yearly rise in figures. During 1940 1,328 juveniles were prosecuted in connection with 1,241 indictable offences, compared with 746 juveniles for 735 indictable offences in 1939.'[11]

Some children protested in their defence that items taken from bombsites were never likely to be claimed, since often the inhabitants had been killed. On several occasions children even reported the discovery of dead bodies whilst in the process of stealing from bombed-out houses. Some crimes were also blamed on children when they were actually the work of more experienced adult criminals. Nevertheless, police constables maintained that it was relatively easy to judge whether or not property had been targeted by juveniles or adults. Children tended to steal money, food, clothes and cigarettes, whereas adult crooks also stole jewellery, silver cutlery and other valuables. Moreover, the latter usually had a ready market for their stolen goods. City children did not become Artful Dodgers as such, since most stole at random rather than to order. The Blitz also offered opportunities for juvenile crime that would not usually be present in peacetime. Nearly all working-class families were short of money, food and clothing, and a large number of children genuinely believed that by stealing from bombed-out houses, in particular, they were helping their families to survive.[12]

Obviously, this was no excuse for criminal activity in a court of law, but in an environment where children were surrounded by nightly destruction and possessed the knowledge that many people would no longer have any use for their belongings, childlike logic prevailed. Children were naturally curious about the war and eager to find out more about the enemy, they also expressed a certain amount of glee when enemy pilots were shot down, as one mother noted in her diary:

M came over last Sunday, the first time since the blitz started. Dick gave her a bit of Messerschmitt and she told us of a policeman she was speaking to whose job it is to watch for falling aeroplanes. H has to immediately jump on his bicycle and go to the spot and he says that he has never yet beaten the boys to a wreck. They are always there first and the other day he got to a crashed aeroplane to find the little devils inside it. One boy took a scarf from a dead German pilot's neck.[13]

There was also an increasing recognition that deprived social conditions in industrial areas often gave rise to juvenile crime, particularly malnutrition. This issue was debated at some length in the House of Commons:

Every doctor who has practiced in an industrial area knows that malnutrition is a common thing and that although children look fairly well in the summer they go down at the first shot in winter. Instead of just a short common cold, they develop bronchitis and broncho-pneumonia. That occurs year after year, and yet these children hold on to life tenaciously when at seventeen or eighteen, they have to bear the whole burden of industry. It is remarkable to me that they behave so well and keep the laws of the land as they do after having had such a bad start. [14]

Clearly the press claims of the existence of a new wartime breed of Artful Dodgers were exaggerated out of all proportion, but though Britain was not breeding a new generation of Artful Dodgers in the Blitz, by keeping the gates of city schools closed, children were in increasing danger of growing up without an adequate moral compass. It was imperative, therefore, for local city councils and the central government's Board of Education to reach a decision about re-opening schools for city youngsters throughout the country.

Notes

1   Research conducted for BBC television documentary *Hop, Skip and Jump*, first broadcast 17 January 2011.
2   'The Question of Reopening Schools' in *Journal of Education*, 3 November 1939, vol. LXXIV, no. 1921, p. 377.
3   National Archive, Conference on Evacuation, 22 January 1940, PRO/ ED/136/125.

4 Ibid.

5 Hansard House of Commons Parliamentary Debates, 5th Series, oral answers, 2 May 1940, col, 885.

6 The views of the Archbishop of Canterbury on the issue of evacuation recorded in 'Evacuation Notes' in *Journal of Education*, vol. LXXIV, no. 1921, 3 November 1939, p. 377.

7 National Archive PRO/MAF/186/16. Outline of the defence regulations pertaining to the Ministry of Agriculture and Fisheries, and statistics concerning child labour.

8 The Royal London Hospital Nurses League, review no. xi, 1942, p. 14.

9 The Royal College of Nursing, *History of Nursing Journal*, vol. 3, no. 3, 1990, pp. 44–7.

10 *The Times*, 18 November 1940.

11 'Juvenile offenders in Manchester' in *Journal of Education*, vol. LXXVIII, no. 2008, 4 July 1941, p. 7.

12 *Secrets of the Blitz*, produced by Steve Humphries, Testimony Films, first broadcast 22 January 2011.

13 Garfield, S., *We Are At War* (2005), p. 386.

14 Hansard House of Commons Parliamentary Debates, 5th Series, 30 June 1942, vol. 385, col. 124.

4

Education in the Rubble

*T*he prospect of educating children amongst city bombsites once the bombing began filled most officials with horror. Aside from the fact that there were no air-raid shelters in schools, there were no teachers left in the cities to teach them. They had been required to escort and reside with their evacuee pupils in the reception areas. Social worker Eileen Potter described her thoughts on the situation in her diary:

Wednesday 27th September

Plans are in the air for the re-opening of schools on a small scale. Groups of children are to be collected from the streets and set to play, or to occupy themselves in some educational way. Suggestion is made that we might like to join in. The idea does not appeal to me at all as I have no gift for amusing children en masse (even in small numbers) or for keeping them in order. In fact, the idea depresses me more than anything else which has happened since the war started, but presently it occurs to me that it will probably fall through. (In the upshot, the working of the scheme is left to trained teachers only, and it finally has to be abandoned in favour of house to house visiting, as the government refuses to countenance the assembling together of more than six children at once in the evacuated areas).[1]

A mother of four children also recorded in her concerns in her diary:

> It seems to me that much more reflection should have been given to this
> evacuation business. I'm not absolutely sure of its being a good thing, for
> it seems to me that the psychological disruption of evacuation may well
> be equal to the evils of living under war conditions. All the money that
> was spent on evacuation could well have been devoted to making schools
> safe and the building of adequate air raid shelters.[2]

Following much deliberation a few schools reopened in London in December 1939, but the Board of Education did not officially sanction the reopening of city schools until the spring of 1940. The government had not wanted to encourage evacuated children to return to the cities but recognised the desperate need to provide education for the children who had remained, since these represented more than 50 per cent of the child population. Furthermore, by December 1939 so many evacuated children had returned to cities to join those children who had remained, that most city teachers were superfluous in reception areas. These teachers were, therefore, recalled to the cities and retired teachers were brought out of retirement to fill the gap left by those who had joined the armed forces. School buildings, however, were unsafe in virtually all local authorities. The Air Raid Precautions Act of 1937 had allocated grants to local authorities for the protection of the general public. Yet within three months of the act being passed the government lifted all expenditure for the safeguarding of schoolchildren from the ambit of the act, claiming that schoolchildren did not form part of the general public! In England and Wales 270 local education authorities were thus confronted with a moral obligation to provide air-raid protection for schoolchildren, but without the necessary funding to do so.

Faced with the prospect of reopening city schools in 1940 the Board of Education came under increasing pressure to ensure the safety of schoolchildren. School buildings were extremely vulnerable at any rate because they contained huge glass windows. Therefore, the first task for teachers was to protect children from potential glass splinters by covering windows with muslin and fine mesh wire. A makeshift shelter consisting of strong sturdy tables was also constructed in one corner of the classroom. The cheapest method of providing some protection for schoolchildren relied on the conversion of downstairs cloakrooms and lavatories. These were sandbagged and the windows were bricked up in an effort to form a secure shelter. But none of these precautions offered any real protection from a direct hit and a lack of proper shelters for schools prompted Sir George Tomlinson, president of the Association of Education Committees, and Sir Percival Sharp, secretary of the association, to write an open letter to Sir John Anderson. They pointed out what they considered to be flagrant breaches of the original Air Raid Precautions Act:

> I was in all the negotiations and all the discussions with the government on Air Raid Precautions. and at no time was it ever suggested, at no time did it become within our knowledge, that a distinction was to be made between the protection of children within schools, and the protection of the general public, nor was the suggestion ever made that there should be a difference in the financial arrangements.
>
> We do not question your power to issue this order. The power of Ministers to issue orders which have the effect of abrogating or even altering the significance of Acts of Parliament of which your 'order' is an instance, has been the subject of severe condemnation by the highest legal authority. But we question the righteousness of your action. It is one thing to have power. It is another thing to use it unrighteously.[3]

Sir John Anderson, however, had firmly believed that all city children would be evacuated to areas of relative safety in the country and city schools would therefore not require air-raid shelters. The problem stemmed from the fact that the government's dispersal policy had not been the resounding success he had originally anticipated. Local authorities were thus left to their own devices in terms of providing air-raid precautions. Even where schools were afforded some protection this was minimal. Arguments against the mass reopening of city schools continued to rage and, as one councillor in Liverpool stressed, 'it is better to have an uneducated child than one in the cemetery'.[4]

The problem of providing an education for remaining city children was compounded by the large-scale return of evacuees to the cities, so government ministers embarked on a new propaganda campaign in an effort to stem the tide. A poster was issued depicting a cartoon of Hitler hiding amongst the trees in a woodland area where mothers were shown picnicking with their children. The poster contained a speech bubble coming from Hitler's mouth saying 'send them back mother', with the obvious suggestion that mothers who were bringing their children back to the cities were playing right into the hands of the Nazi leader. In an effort to prevent more children from returning to cities the Minister of Health made a personal appeal to parents:

> You are among the many fathers and mothers who wisely took advantage of the government's scheme to send their children to the country. I am sorry to learn that some parents are now bringing their children back. I am writing to ask you not to do this. This is not easy, because family life has always been the strength and pride of Britain. But I feel it my duty to remind you that brining children back to the congested towns is to put them at danger of death or what is perhaps worse maiming for life. You will have noticed that the enemy is changing his tactics. He is now concentrating heavier air raids on one or two towns at a time, leaving others alone for the moment. Nobody knows which town he will attack next so don't be lulled into a false sense of security if your home district has been having a quieter time lately. Remember that in April over six hundred children under the age of sixteen were killed and over five hundred were seriously injured in air raids. So keep your children where they are in the reception areas. Don't bring them back even for a little while. This is your duty to the children themselves, to the A.R.P. services in your home town, to those who are working so hard for them in the country, and to the nation. Please read this message as the sincere words of a friend both to you and the little ones.[5]

This appeal was written with honourable motives and genuine concern, but it was estimated that over 90 per cent of evacuees had already returned to the cities long before it was published or read by anyone.

Individual city councils developed their own strategies for the education of their children and much depended on the efficiency and determination of the councils concerned. In London's East Ham thirteen schools were afforded air-raid protection in December 1939, but the *Journal of Education* belatedly published the fact that 'hope was expressed that this would not be the signal for the wholesale return of evacuees'.[6]

In Sheffield, where one part of the city was considered to be an evacuation area, teachers developed a system of home schooling. In September 1939 there was a total role of 61,623 schoolchildren registered at the school departments of Sheffield and a further 430 nursery-age children, yet only 5,000 of these were evacuated to parts of Nottinghamshire and Leicestershire. By appealing to parents and local residents for accommodation, Sheffield education authority was able to establish an efficient home-school teaching system. In total, 3–4,000 privately owned properties were in use at any given time and, within six days of the outbreak of war, 5,372 groups, each consisting of eight to twelve children, were being educated in private homes, factory basements and garages across the city. A school inspector recorded in 1942 that 'the magnitude of the task can best be judged by the fact that nearly all the children joined in, and over 1,500 Head and Assistant Teachers were regularly in action.'[7] On average, children received five hours' tuition a week and the Board of Education quickly endorsed the home school system. It remained the only experimental system of education to be initiated by teachers during the war and the Sheffield example was followed by other cities such as Manchester, Liverpool and Birmingham. In London's West Ham home teaching was established using 163 houses and fourteen small halls. A Mr T. Letherby, reporting on the scheme, stated that, 'one and a half hours daily instruction is little enough, but there is no doubt that the boys and girls have derived benefit from it. In their small classes they seem eager and happy, and many of them express regret when their short period is finished.'[8]

In addition to the fact that city children enjoyed home schooling – being taught in small groups they received more individual attention – teachers were able to be more innovative. In truth, it can be said that home schooling generated its liveliest vitality when it discarded time-honoured classroom methods and approaches – which, in any case, were inappropriate – and made first-hand enquiries and investigations. In many cases the development of new and hitherto untried techniques began. Programmes varied greatly in character, some were determined with caution and some with courage, but always with honesty and common sense. It seemed to the observer that for the first time many subjects of instruction, not least the more formal ones, came into realistic contact with the child's environment and consequently assumed a new and potent significance.[9]

In the sense that home schools concentrated on basic subjects such as arithmetic and English they were not particularly radical. However, the way these subjects were taught marked a real departure from traditional teaching methods. Arithmetic was taught in relation to the weighing of food for instance, and English composition in relation to a child's home experiences. Teachers were able to take children on educational trips to water and electricity companies, canal wharves, botanical gardens, railway stations and museums. Small groups enabled more experimentation and, as these same groups contained children of varying ages, older pupils encouraged the younger ones in much the same way as they did in a normal family framework.

Nevertheless, not all city home school systems were as successful as the Sheffield model. It can also be argued that they were exploited in some cities, and used as an excuse for authorities not to provide air-raid shelters for schools in others. They were also limited in terms of the amount of instruction hours they were able to offer, and levels of childhood illiteracy were increasing in major cities. It was not uncommon, for example, to find 13-year-old boys in cities such as London, Manchester, Liverpool and Birmingham who were unable to read at all.

Furthermore, although the Board of Education gave the go-ahead for schools to reopen in 1940, many did not have enough available places and a proportion of children were still left to roam the streets. Official concern and disquiet over the lack of air-raid precautions in city schools also resulted in a policy of voluntary school attendance. As Sir Percy Harris, MP for Bethnal Green south-west, observed of city schools:

> In the first few months of the war there was no provision for education at all. Schools were closed and children were running wild about the streets, and no serious attempt was made to do anything. Such were the difficulties that finally we had a voluntary system – voluntary attendance. It was the most comic experiences that I have ever come across: children going in and out of school as they pleased, attending sometimes for a day or two if they felt so inclined. There is much credit due to those children who did go to school of their own accord.[10]

There were various rationales behind the notion of voluntary attendance. In Bradford and a few other northern cities many children could not get to school because of transport problems. Footwear was another issue that dictated a child's ability to attend classes. With children in the same family often sharing footwear it was common to see varying attendance rates, especially on cold or wet days. On dry days most children simply attended school barefoot.

The demands of war had resulted in an extreme shortage of leather, canvas and rubber shoes. Substandard repairs in some areas had compounded the problem and children were often away from school for weeks while repairs took place. For example, the number of absences due to a lack of boots or clothes during the month of September 1942 in Bristol varied in sixteen districts from twenty eight to 860. Although, according to the Board of Trade, wartime production of children's shoes had not fallen from pre-war levels except in the case of plimsolls and Wellington boots.[11] Much of the problem stemmed from the fact that children's shoes were being made of very poor quality leather that fell apart after a few weeks, and it was no longer possible to prolong the life of shoes with boots or plimsolls. Teachers in Birmingham, Liverpool, Manchester and London all reported that children were turning up for lessons in bare feet or failing to turn up at all. The distribution of new footwear was severely constrained by the lack of raw materials. Schools were also experiencing fuel shortages and the combination of these problems prompted the publication of a provocative article in the *Journal of Education*:

The bitterly cold weather of this Christmas time has brought to many thinking minds the wretched plight of the poorest of our children, ill clad and ill shod. The bombing of so many large towns has resulted in the immediate evacuation of large numbers of children in a state of destitution. For their distressful needs there is no remedy beyond voluntary effort supplemented by the provisions of the Public Assistance Board and the Unemployed Assistance Board. How blind are our Central Administrators? How unfeeling they seem to be. They chop logic about the functions of these two Committees: about the powers that these Committees possess: how their formulae should cover all the needs of the family and so on. In the meantime needy children are shivering outdoors in icy blasts: indoors where fuel deliveries have broken down. Cannot our legislators; our administrators learn anything from the enemy who look upon children as their first and most valuable heritage: as their first care? Cannot they imagine the feelings of the honest poor who see their children enduring such keen suffering? Cannot they realise that their cold blooded administration is nicely calculated to manufacture enemies of the state? The cold indifference of the Government and, indeed of the Board of Education to the plight of so many needy children is startling.[12]

An analysis of parliamentary debates, however, reveals that government ministers were fully aware of the plight of needy children, and were doing their utmost to resolve the problem. Their efforts were frustrated and often completely thwarted by a severe shortage of raw materials and by a lack of local authority co-operation. Each committee and each local authority shifted

Children of an eastern suburb of London, made homeless by the random bombs of the Nazi night raiders, waiting outside the wreckage of what was their home, September 1940. (*New York Times* Paris Bureau Collection/Wikimedia Commons)

responsibility from department to department, and urgent and genuine claims for assistance rarely received a prompt response.

A lack of clothing and footwear was not the largest cause of school absenteeism in cities, however, neither was it the main reason behind the idea of voluntary attendance. The matter was simple. Most city schools did not have air-raid shelters. Local education authorities believed that if parents were made aware of this stark fact and voluntarily chose to send their children to school, then the onus for child safety was on the parents rather than on the education authority. The latter would be partially absolved from blame, therefore, should tragedies occur – which they did. For example, on 20 January 1943 the Germans staged daylight raids on London that resulted in a number of bombs being dropped on Sandhurst Road School in Catford, east London. In total thirty-eight pupils between the ages of 5 and 12 were killed alongside six of their teachers. There were other daylight raids on London and major cities of a similar nature with similar results. The risks associated with sending children to city schools were obvious, and education officials understandably did not want to shoulder the responsibility of such risks. There is considerable evidence to demonstrate that each city education authority attempted to do all that it could to prepare teachers and pupils in an attempt to prevent such disasters. Teacher Rhoda Edmonds recalled:

> Everyone that worked for the authority had to learn first aid and we were all tested. The course was very basic and the test was easy. When I did my test, the examiner in charge, he just asked me where the pressure points were on the body. Once I told him where they were he issued me with my first aid certificate. Looking back though, I suppose it was all I needed to know.[13]

In addition to the usual gas mask drills, teachers were also required to simulate scenes and situations where they and their pupils might be disorientated as a result of bombing or subsequent fires. In major cities around the country, therefore, there were hysterical scenes of laughter as children practised these drills. Children were taught to lie on the floor on their stomachs and grab the ankles of the child in front of them to form a long snake of bodies. Then they were told to keep their faces to the ground to avoid breathing in any smoke or gas and wriggle out of the classroom in order to escape the building. Teachers were required to boil several kettles of water to produce enough steam to imitate the smoke. Such practice runs were often met with shrieks of laughter and giggles from the pupils while teachers did their utmost to explain the seriousness and necessity of the drills. In schools that lacked any form of air-raid shelter it was commonplace for the head teacher to arrange for children to run to the garden shelters of private householders. Each shelter was allotted a number of children depending on its size, and practice runs were made each day. When the number of shelters were too few, head teachers frequently organised the digging of ditches and children were allotted places in the ditch. In the event, gas masks were not needed, but in major cities whole schools were obliterated by the Luftwaffe, though as one man who attended school in London recalled.

> Sometimes just part of the school was bombed, and often, if the building was considered to be safe we just carried on going to school. The worst thing was sitting down in the morning to begin lessons and counting the number of empty desks in the classroom. We lost a lot of friends that way.[14]

Iris Williams remembered when her school was bombed to ruins:

> I was at the Castle Street school for a year before it was bombed. I had just got a new gym kit and some new material for my needlework lessons. We used to have air raid warnings and rush to some shelters that had been dug under a park. I always wanted them to happen in the algebra lesson because I hated algebra. Anyway, when the sirens sounded we would rush to the shelters with our gas masks and our tuck boxes – we always remembered to take our food. Anyway, on the night of 24th November 1940 the school was very badly bombed and it was impossible for us to go back. The school was just a pile of rubble, some of it was still standing but nothing was left of the classrooms. We children all thought that we would have a long time off school and we were looking forward to not going until at least after the Christmas holidays. But our parents received a letter instructing us to attend a local boy's school. It seemed quite funny to us girls at the time to be attending a boy's school, but we just got on with it.[15]

Even in Wales, where children were supposedly safer, there were incidents of widespread bombing, especially Cardiff and the surrounding dockland

BRISTOL EDUCATION COMMITTEE

Commercial School Certificate

This is to Certify that

Iris Williams

born the 14th day of September in the year 1927
has completed an approved full course of Commercial
Education and has satisfied the Examiners that she has
reached the standard shown in the following subjects.

*Group I. Arithmetic & Accounts, English,
Geography, Shorthand, Typewriting.*

Group II. Commerce, French, History,

*Group III. Art, English Literature,
Physical Training, Scripture.*

Signed on behalf of the Bristol Education Committee

J. Williams

Chairman

Signed on behalf of the Union of Educational Institutions
(Assessors for the Examination)

Iris Williams' central school certificate awarded in 1943. This was one of the last central school certificates to be awarded in Britain because they were abolished under the Butler Education Act of 1944. (Reproduced by kind permission of Iris Williams) settlements of Barry. During one of the worst raids on 2 January 1941, bombers missed the docks and showered their high explosives on houses and schools:

> More than sixty civilians were killed in the Riverside suburb within the first half an hour of the raid that had started soon after sunset, at 5pm. Seven mourners at a funeral party which had decided not to take shelter were killed when a land mine hit a house, throwing a car a hundred yards. In a nearby street a rescue party dug for six hours to rescue a six year old child trapped under the staircase where he had been sheltering. Throughout the rescue the boy was reported to have sung 'God Save the King.' He had learned from his father, a coal miner, that when men were buried underground, they kept 'singing and singing,' and he said that the National Anthem was the only song he knew all the words to.[16]

The lack of adequate schooling in cities prompted several entrepreneurs to start small private schools. For a small fee they would take in as many children as they could house and offer them a range of academic subjects. However, the tuition in these schools was often substandard and frequently run by charlatans with no teaching qualifications whatsoever. Most were closed down within weeks of opening.

A more successful route to learning both in schools and at home was provided by the BBC within its school broadcasting programme. Subjects included world history, literacy, play writing and drama, practical gardening, science, biology, current affairs, religion and music. Of particular value to city children was the home listening service. This programme provided structured learning in a variety of subjects for children who were studying at home, with or without supervision. Most families had a wireless and for a short while each day children were able to gather around and listen to broadcasts that were directly aimed at improving their knowledge and connection with the world around them. There were stories about life in Canada, life on the road, life in the country, life with Indians, life under the sea and life in other parts of Great Britain. Programmes educated children as best they could about their everyday surroundings and introduced them to a world of imagination and wonder. Furthermore, programme presenters were often male and down to earth characters. For instance, children were informed about exploits of Canadian lumberjacks from a lorry driver called Alf.[17]

By this stage the long-awaited camp schools were up and running on the outskirts of some major cities. In certain areas, such as the suburbs of Birmingham, they were primarily used to accommodate children who had quite literally been bombed out of their homes. In others, such as those that were built outside London, they were generally used to accommodate pre-existing schools. They were viewed by government officials as an educational experiment and records suggest that they were in fact, from an educational standpoint, a resounding success. However, though children who attended camp schools certainly fared better than those who were privately billeted, they still failed to thrive adequately in terms of normal childhood development. Evidence from camp schools reveals that the pupils seemed reasonably happy and educationally sound, but their average height and weight measurements did not match those of children who had remained in the cities.

Educational attainments in camp schools, however, were above the national average. Moreover, while city children undoubtedly enjoyed better emotional health and more normal child development patterns, they had suffered on the education front. Literacy tests conducted in 1943 demonstrated an alarming rise in the numbers of children who could not read at all and a distinct rise in those who could not read fluently. In 1924, for example, the average London boy of 13 misspelt a word every time he wrote a dozen lines of composition; in 1943, one word in six lines was miss-spelt. While children were still able to write lively and intelligent compositions, spelling was definitely worse than corresponding pupils in 1924.[18]

Knowledge of maths, history and geography had also declined, particularly in city children, which was not surprising given their enormous educational upheavals and the distinct lack of education in some areas for months on end. Even when some semblance of normal education was established in cities, the disruption to lessons and exam schedules caused by bombing made it impossible for children to absorb everyday facts and figures. Most were too tired following a nights, bombing raid to pay any attention to lessons, and it was not uncommon for children to fall asleep at their desks. Indeed, it was remarkable for any child who lived through the Blitz to attain normal levels of academic achievement. The decline in wartime educational standards did, however, prompt a series of intense debates within government circles. Furthermore, the president of the Board of Education, Mr R.A. Butler, responded to these debates promptly and pragmatically by advocating widespread reform of the British education system. Subsequently, there were long-running battles between those ministers in favour of reform and those who opposed any form of change. Despite objections the Butler Education Act was passed in 1944. This legislation effectively raised the school-leaving age to 16, divided primary, secondary and further education institutes, and implemented administrative reform measures. By providing free education for all children, the act also laid the foundations for a new post-war education system.

Notes

1 Garfield, S., *We Are At War* (2005), p. 42.
2 Ibid., p. 116.
3 Tomlinson, G. and Sharp, P., 'Open letter to Sir John Anderson' in *Journal of Education*, vol. LXXV, no. 1935, 9 February 1940, p. 110.
4 'Educational Administration' in *Journal of Education*, 15 December 1939, vol. LXXIV, no. 1927, p. 502.
5 Ministry of Health Circular HMSO, June 1940.
6 'Educational Administration' in *Journal of Education*, 15 December 1939, vol. LXXIV, no. 1927, p. 502.
7 Sheffield City Archives, ref. CA/43/1, Report of HMI Elementary Schooling in Wartime, 28 April 1942.
8 'Home Teaching' in *Journal of Education*, vol. LXXV, no. 1935, p. 116.
9 Sheffield City Archives, ref. CA/43/1, Report of HMI Elementary Schooling in Wartime, 28 April 1942.
10 Harris, P., Hansard House of Commons Parliamentary Debates, 5th Series, 16 June 1942, col. 1458.
11 Titmuss, R., *Problems of Social Policy* (1950), pp. 421–2.
12 Sharp, P., 'Boots for the Bairns' in *Journal of Education*, vol. LXXVII, no. 1982, 3 January 1941.
13 Oral history interview: Edmonds, Rhoda, April 2011.
14 Oral history interview: E.A.S., August 2000.
15 Oral history interview: Iris Williams, 17 May 2011.
16 Gardiner, J., *The Blitz: The British Under Attack* (2010), p. 269.
17 Hickman, T., *What Did You Do in the War Auntie?* (1995), p. 79.
18 Titmuss, R., *Problems of Social Policy* (1950), p. 408–9.

5

Childhood Epidemics

A ccording to school log books, surviving medical records and oral history testimonies, childhood epidemics were the chief cause of infant mortality during the Second World War. They far surpassed the impact of bombing in terms of the number of fatalities – although figures were initially difficult to contain.

The most prevalent childhood epidemics that rampaged through the nation during the Blitz were diphtheria, tuberculosis, measles, polio, mumps, scarlet fever and whooping cough; all of which flourished in overcrowded conditions with poor sanitation and hygiene. To compound this, those who were particularly ill-nourished and weak in constitution could offer little resistance to these diseases. It was no surprise, therefore, that children who were living in extreme poverty were more likely to succumb to any prevalent epidemic. At least two-thirds of all children fell into this category. Even before the war, there was a growing recognition that the impact of the 1930s Depression had taken its toll on the health of British children. Concerns were raised in the House of Commons with regard to their physical wellbeing, and particularly those who were living in the north of England. In Tyneside and Durham it was estimated that the numbers of undernourished children had risen by 10 per cent between 1935 and 1938. School inspections had also revealed that there were three times as many undernourished children living in these areas than in London and the whole of the south-east,[1] although a few southern counties such as Sussex also contained poor areas. Poverty was by no means restricted to inner-city areas, but by virtue of population numbers and demography undernourished children were more often city born and bred. In the

House of Commons, MP Dr Thomas sympathetically described the typical undernourished child as being:

> pale, with a flabby face and red nose, with no overcoat and his hands tucked into his sleeves going to school on a cold winter's morning after his breakfast of tea, bread and jam. Closer examination by anyone – it does not need any medical knowledge – would show that he often has nasal catarrh, breathes badly, is flat-chested and knock-kneed. He is a common sight – dull and listless at his lessons and slow at his play.[2]

In addition to long-standing undernourishment, the level of overcrowding experienced in both the evacuation and reception areas clearly had an impact on the incidence of disease. Despite the distribution of public health pamphlets that stated 'coughs and sneezes spread diseases', the situation was further compounded by the perpetual blackout conditions, since these required householders to close and black out their windows to deter enemy bombers, which resulted in poor ventilation. Obviously, the Blitz increased overcrowding because whole families along with their neighbours were huddled together night after night in packed Underground shelters, Anderson shelters and any other appropriate structure to shield themselves from enemy bombing. Thus between the end of 1940 and the end of 1941 there was a massive increase in the number of deaths from infectious diseases. Whooping cough had claimed 678 deaths in 1940, compared to 2,383 in 1941. The number of deaths from measles had also risen from 857 cases in 1940 to 1,145 cases in 1941. In addition to these and other childhood illnesses, cases of tuberculosis were also increasing on a yearly basis.

In terms of wartime infectious diseases, however, diphtheria was public enemy number one. Diphtheria was renowned as 'the child killer', and was responsible for more child fatalities between the ages of 4 and 10 years old than any other. It was possible to immunise children against the disease and Ministry of Health policy aimed to immunise at least 75 per cent of children before the end of 1941. Yet in England and Wales in that year alone there were 2,641 deaths from diphtheria, and the government had fallen severely short of its immunisation target. By the end of 1941 only 33 per cent of the child population had been immunised against the disease, instead of the proposed target of 75 per cent. Central government policy directives had made concerted efforts to improve public health and combat infectious diseases, but in their effort to improve the nation's health they were met with severe and entrenched opposition from local health authorities. Even though experience in Canada and the United States of America had already demonstrated that by immunising all children under the age of 15 years it was possible not only to reduce fatalities but also totally eradicate the disease. British resistance towards immunisation programmes was in part financially motivated, since local authorities were reluctant to pay for the staff required to implement such programmes, but adverse publicity about the efficacy and safety of vaccines also played a role in restricting the initial uptake of immunisation against diphtheria.

In 1941 there were 50,000 recorded sufferers of diphtheria in England and Wales, but this number was not that dissimilar to 1916 figures which recorded 53,000 sufferers of the disease in England and Wales. In terms of public health, a drop of 3,000 sufferers in two and a half decades could not be described as marked progress. The death rate from diphtheria had fallen, from 5,300 in 1916 to 2,641 in 1941, but Ministry of Health officials were clearly fighting a losing battle in their attempt to eradicate the disease. Strong appeals were issued to parents in an effort to persuade them to attend local health authority clinics and present their children for immunisation, but they seemed to be falling on deaf ears. An indifferent parental response to such appeals, however, was not entirely to blame for low immunisation rates, and much depended on the willingness of local authorities to comply with Ministry of Health directives.

For the duration of the war local health authorities fought their own private and individual battles with central government. Local authorities, particularly in reception areas, had been dismayed by the large numbers of evacuees that had flooded in without adequate prior consultation, and faced with limited health and education resources many officials in these authorities resolved to resist any further instructions from Whitehall. In fact, by 1941 Ministry of Health officials recognised that, having offloaded responsibility for child welfare firmly onto overstretched local authorities with the implementation of evacuation schemes, it was time for them to assume the reins once more. Renewed and more robust immunisation initiatives were a clear indication that central government was now firmly back in the policy driving seat. Although health workers in evacuation areas were surprised to discover that, initially, no immunisation programmes existed for city children because it was assumed they would all be living in the country.

To compound these problems, publicity surrounding the issue of immunisation during the early war years was not all favourable, as a number of children died of diphtheria following their inoculations. These children were unlucky enough to have contracted the disease a few days after their inoculation and before immunity had been properly established. There were others who developed encephalitis following inoculation and also died. These cases were rare, but when they occurred received a great deal of attention and engendered fear amongst the general public. To give an example of the rarity of post-inoculation and vaccination encephalitis in the first four months of 1940, there were six reported cases – three of whom were serving soldiers.[3]

Despite the low incidence of encephalitis, existing cases were seized upon for propaganda purposes by groups of ignorant but loquacious adults who were highly suspicious of the whole process of inoculation and vaccination. The most vociferous of these apprehensive and dubious groups was the Anti-Vaccination League, who launched an aggressive advertising campaign in an attempt to thwart all immunisation programmes. Subsequently they ensured that advertisements were published in the national press containing distressing images of children who were suffering from encephalitis, and these were accompanied by a series of scaremongering articles. Fabricated case histories were included in some publications and newspaper articles which highlighted the numerous dangers supposedly associated with all forms of inoculation. Members of the league genuinely believed that with improved nutrition and hygiene disease could be eradicated without inoculation, as children and adults would build up their own immunity naturally over a period of time. They argued that vaccines were unsafe, and that since immunised children often still contracted the disease the risk of inoculation far outweighed the risk of the disease. Some members even believed that vaccination actively destroyed a child's ability to produce immunity. The league also objected to smallpox vaccinations, studiously ignoring the fact that they had long since proved their value. In terms of thwarting improvements to child health, members of the league achieved limited success. Their views were irresponsible to say the least, but they were bolstered by a few odd and old-fashioned members of the medical profession and ensured that the issue remained controversial for at least the first three years of the war.

Ministry of Health officials did not deviate from their policy goals but appeared to be somewhat bemused by the existence of opposition towards policies that were clearly for the benefit of all. The government stance remained resolute, since ministers had taken advice from renowned medical experts; primarily from Canada, where immunisation had achieved spectacular results both in terms of reducing the incidence and fatalities due to diphtheria. They had rigorously examined the evidence and concluded that the most responsible course of action was to actively encourage immunisation for all children under the age of 15. Therefore, a widespread publicity campaign was launched in conjunction with the Central Council for Health Education, which aimed to persuade all parents to bring their children to the clinics for the relevant injections as a matter of urgency.

The Anti-Vaccination League undermined this process and many parents refused to have their children inoculated on numerous occasions, citing the perverse literature of the league as the reason for their objections. But the activities of the league were mitigated to some extent by astute medical officers, who argued that they were unable to accept the signature of mothers as grounds for objection to immunisation, and insisted on having the father's signature as head of the household. Since many fathers were away serving in the armed forces, or were at work during the times when inoculations were being carried out, it was extremely difficult – if not well-nigh impossible – for some mothers to obtain the father's signature. Certainly a number of children were inoculated against their mother's wishes and perhaps against the wishes of both parents.

Aside from the activities of the Anti-Vaccination League, the Ministry of Health had other problems to contend with. Of the parents who were willing to have their children inoculated, some turned up at health clinics to discover that their local authorities were less than enthusiastic about inoculation programmes. Although the ministry supplied the toxoid at a cost of approximately £13,500 a year, local authorities were still required to foot the bill of supplying medical staff to administer the injections and to keep appropriate records. In view of the fact that public opinion was not always in favour of inoculation programmes it was relatively easy for local authorities to neglect their responsibilities in this respect. The constant ebb and flow of children between evacuation and reception areas did nothing to help matters. Some children invariably 'slipped through the net', even in areas where programmes were reasonably efficient.

Children living in cities were experiencing the overcrowding of shelters and bombed-out rubble of the Blitz, and were undoubtedly more likely to catch diphtheria than any other group. In part, this increased susceptibility was due to cramped living conditions and bombed water pipes. Associated problems with obtaining clean water naturally resulted in poor hygiene and an increased likelihood of childhood epidemics. Yet health authorities in major cities saw

An example of the rubble on London's streets caused by the Blitz: Hallam Street and Duchess Street, Westminster, London, 1940. (City of Westminster Archive Centre/ Wikimedia Commons)

no reason to establish inoculation programmes, since in theory these children were supposed to be living in safer, rural reception areas. Furthermore, they argued, most injections were administered within the school environment and since schools were closed in evacuation areas there was no effective way of establishing a reliable method of mass inoculation.

Using such arguments to resist the implementation of immunisation strategies however, did not really hold water, because the best time to inoculate children was during their infancy. Research and practical experience in other countries had demonstrated that inoculation was most effective if administered to babies before their 1st birthday. There was some suggestion in the House of Commons that information about inoculation should be distributed to parents by the registrar of births. In this way all parents would receive vital information as soon as they registered their child's name and details, though Ministry of Health officials were reluctant to take this action on the grounds that administratively the process could prove to be complicated and insensitive. It was deemed inappropriate to distribute information about diphtheria prevention within an environment where some people would also be required to register deaths from the disease. Yet by 1942 ministers were desperate to find a way to increase inoculation rates. On an average day diphtheria cases still occupied approximately 4,000 hospital beds and MPs were demanding that fresh and more vigorous efforts should be made to combat the disease.

Accepting the challenge with increased vigor, the Ministry of Health adopted a two-pronged approach. The first was aimed at parents and took the form of a strongly worded publicity campaign. Health promotion leaflets, posters and newspaper articles, which emanated from Whitehall at this time, all reminded parents in no uncertain terms of the dreadful horrors that could befall their children if they failed to get them inoculated. The second approach was aimed at local authorities and took the form of aggressive persuasion. Local authorities were gradually cajoled and convinced by the ministry that inoculation would, in the long term, save them considerable amounts of money by reducing the costs of hospital and nursing services. However the biggest boost to the new inoculation campaign came from an unexpected quarter.

In April 1942 the British Advertising Association took the unprecedented step of recommending that all newspapers and magazines should refuse to publish any material that emanated from the Anti-Vaccination League. This extraordinary decision was taken by prominent members of the association who believed that it was time to come down off the fence with regard to the inoculation issue and act in the public's best interest. Medical opinion was overwhelming in support of this course of action, and by this stage in the war medical professionals from Canada and America had also crossed the Atlantic to advise the British government on health care policy in this respect and aid the British fight against specific childhood diseases.

The Anti-Vaccination League did not succumb quietly to this move however, and their protagonists within government circles lobbied long and hard to get the British Advertising Association decision overturned. Mr Viant asked the Minister of Health whether he was:

> aware of the widespread opposition to diphtheria immunization; that this opposition has considerable support from medical practitioners; and whether, as the question is a controversial one and Parliament has never expressed any opinion on advertisements relating to opinions adverse to this inoculation, he will give instructions to stop the issue of advice, such as that recently given to the Advertising Association, to assist in the boycott of the advertisements of the Anti-Vaccination League?[4]

Clearly since the Advertising Association's initiative had not stemmed from government intervention there was no need for the government to do anything at all in this respect. Indeed the Minister stated, 'in reply to an inquiry from the Advertising Association my department wrote that, if the Association decided to recommend newspapers to refuse advertisements designed to discourage the immunization of children against diphtheria they would be working in accordance with government policy.'[5]

There was no question that the Advertising Association's decision with regard to the Anti-Vaccination League did bear fruit. In particular there was noticeable impact on parents with young babies. Whereas only 33 per cent of the whole population in England and Wales had been inoculated against diphtheria by the end of 1941, by the end of 1942 39.6 of all new births had been inoculated and the number was increasing. In Scotland the figure was slightly higher. Certainly 1942 marked a turning point in terms of the battle against diphtheria. Although the incidence of the disease was still rising in some areas, the death rate was actually falling. Statistics were not wholly reliable however, because the registration forms that were used to register deaths from diphtheria did not distinguish between immunised and non-immunised children. Nevertheless, the combination of improved immunity through inoculation and increased resistance to disease, generally as a result of better access to food and milk through school meals and milk programmes did have an impact. The means test, which had previously determined a child's eligibility to receive free milk, was also abandoned as the constant migration of children had rendered means testing a cumbersome and impractical exercise.[6]

Yet the extension of free school milk in some rural areas did have negative consequences for child health. The cases of non-pulmonary tuberculosis increased dramatically throughout the war because children in reception areas were being supplied with untreated milk. In particular, in the smaller reception areas, milk was supplied by producer retailers who had no access to purification plants. Whereas in the cities children fared much better because London dairies, Express dairies and United dairies were responsible for supplying city milk and they only supplied good quality pasteurised milk to the public. Between 1939 and 1942 alone there were at least 13,000 new cases of non-pulmonary tuberculosis and it was conservatively estimated that at least 40 per cent of these were of a bovine origin.

Speaking in the House of Commons in June 1942, Dr Edith Summerskill highlighted the problem:

We have had cheap and free milk, and have encouraged the population to drink milk, with the result I am told, that more milk was drunk last year than ever before. At the same time, we have had an increase in tuberculosis among our children by forty five to one hundred per cent on the peace-time figures. This is not just a coincidence: these facts are related. I do not want to say 'I told you so,' but I believe that during the first two or three months of the war we had a debate on evacuation, and I asked how the children who were evacuated from the towns to the country districts were to be protected.[7]

With regard to the containment of tuberculosis however, the failure to protect country children from infected milk was symptomatic of a number of disastrous health policy decisions. During the early months of the war, for instance, government health officials had decided to close several sanatoriums in preparation for emergency casualties. As a consequence, thousands of newly discharged tuberculosis patients rapidly spread the disease throughout the country. There was also no attempt to keep medical staff from caring for tuberculosis patients one week and patients suffering from other ailments the following week. It was even suggested by the Minister of Health that young girls should be directed to work in sanatoriums because he believed that nurses who cared for tuberculosis patients ran no greater risk of catching the disease working in sanatoriums than working in other hospitals. This was of course total nonsense, as Dr Edith Summerskill was quick to point out:

> I am quoting some of the experts in the country when I say of course these nurses run a greater risk. The Minister should not for one moment consider discussing with the Minister of Labour this matter of having girls directed to tuberculosis sanatoria. The conditions should be improved as, incidentally should the pay. The girls should be allowed to know the danger.[8]

Arguably, parents of evacuated children should also have been informed of the dangers associated with infected milk, but they were not. Crucially, bovine tuberculosis – otherwise known as brucellosis – was far more difficult to treat than the pulmonary version of the disease. Brucellosis attacked the bones, causing severe deformity and fulminating painful joints until the child was totally crippled or the disease proved fatal.[9] But the considerable vested interests in the milk industry hampered government attempts to improve milk hygiene. A White Paper was produced at Westminster on the issue during 1942, but uniformly high standards were not really detectable until the mid-1950s. Even then, children who were accustomed to drinking untreated milk on their own parents' farms still contracted the disease.

Public health successes in the field of tuberculosis were extremely rare during the war and an increasing number of ministers were adamant that until general living conditions were improved the disease could not be eradicated. Most agreed that poor damp housing, overcrowding and malnutrition were the primary problems. Subsequently, Sir William Beveridge was given the task of identifying the root causes of poverty and also of proposing solutions.

Clearly several Ministry of Health policies were undeniably remiss throughout the war. However, some of the problems that were associated with child health centred on the mounting policy gulf between central and local government. Not surprisingly, the Ministry of Health came under severe public and local authority criticism during the early years of the war. Evacuation procedures had not been a great success and the failure to fully equip local authorities for the reception of evacuees had encouraged deep resentment in the reception areas and a widening rift between central and local government. This tenuous relationship deteriorated radically and rapidly during the war.

The tendency later in the war for local authorities to flout central government directives was widespread. Local authority resistance to diphtheria immunisation programmes was a prime example of this inclination. Yet despite this resistance the mortality rate from diphtheria fell by nearly two thirds between 1940 and 1945 and the value of immunisation was confirmed by statistical evidence. Of the 3,346 children who died from diphtheria, 118 were immunised and 3,228 were not.[10] Undoubtedly central government was given a substantial boost in its immunisation campaign from the Advertising Association in 1942, but overcoming local authority opposition remained problematic in some areas for a further two years. Nevertheless, against a background of some otherwise dubious health policy decisions the battle against diphtheria stands out as a shining star of public health policy achievement amidst the chaos and confusion of war.

Table 1: Deaths from diphtheria, measles and whooping cough in England and Wales.

Year	Disease	Males	Females	Persons
1938	diphtheria	1,128	1,049	2,177
	measles	159	150	309
	whooping cough	566	707	1,273
1940	diphtheria	1,254	1,225	2,479
	measles	425	432	857
	whooping cough	326	352	678
1941	diphtheria	1,332	1,309	2,641
	measles	635	510	1,145
	whooping cough	1,013	1,370	2,383

Source: Hansard House of Commons Debates, 5th Series, written answers, 5 May 1942, vol. 379, col. 1229.

Table 2: Diphtheria in Aberdeen.

		1938	1939	1940
Non-immunised children	cases	186	149	114
	deaths	11	7	3
Immunised children	cases	42	16	7
	deaths	0	0	0

Source: Hansard House of Commons Debates, 5th Series, written answers, 13 February 1941, vol. 368, col. 1539.

Table 3: Immunisation against diptheria in England and Wales.

Year	Immunised children under 15
1940 & 1941 (separate figures not available)	2,365,400
1942	1,399,750
1943	1,039,490
1944	561,320

Source: Hansard House of Commons Debates, 5th Series, written answers, 8 November 1945, vol. 415, col. 1571.

Notes

1   Hansard House of Commons Parliamentary Debates, 5th Series, 15 February 1940, vol. 357, col. 939–940.
2   Ibid., 30 June 1942, vol. 385, col. 123.
3   Ibid., 30 April 1940, vol. 357, col. 547.
4   Ibid., 16 April 1942, vol. 379, col. 353.
5   Ibid.
6   The means test was replaced by the Determination of Needs Act in 1941; this introduced an altogether more lenient method of needs assessment. Further changes were made under the National Health Insurance Act in 1941 and the Pensions and Determination of Needs Act in 1943.

7   Hansard House of Commons Parliamentary Debates, 5th Series, 30 June 1942, vol. 385, col. 137.

8   Ibid., col. 136.

9   The last case of brucellosis in Britain was diagnosed at the Bath and Wessex Orthopaedic Hospital in 1972. The 7-year-old boy had been drinking infected untreated milk on his parents' farm in Somerset; he made a successful recovery due to powerful antibiotic medication that was not available during the war.

10 Hansard House of Commons Parliamentary Debates, 5th Series, 8 November 1945, vol. 415, col. 1571.

6

Health and Welfare

With epidemics under control, concern over child health took on a new and broader dimension. Statistically however, there are a few caveats to consider when examining child health and welfare during the war. Poor recordkeeping by a number of overworked doctors obscured and, in some cases, distorted the general picture of health, and a number of records were lost due to bombing raids and social dislocation. Additionally, the overall analysis of the nation's health contained certain anomalies because the healthiest members of the population were away fighting in the armed forces. An examination of wartime parliamentary debates reveals that most government ministers expected child health to deteriorate because of the circumstances of war, and they did their best to counteract this possibility. There was particular concern that bombing raids might seriously disturb water supplies, prompting outbreaks of typhoid and other waterborne diseases. The restrictions on food supplies and the prospect of malnutrition also reared its ugly head. Yet, not withstanding the dubious record keeping in some quarters, it is clear that children – and for the most part adults too – maintained far better levels of health than expected. Good nutrition, rigorous exercise and the eradication of disease were rightly viewed as good building blocks for a fit and healthy nation, but between 1940 and 1941, prompted by the intensity of the Blitz, there was a growing concern with regard to national fitness levels. Senior members of the armed forces were particularly worried, as Major S.J. Parker revealed:

No-one can deny that the future might of a country depended on the quality of its youth, and whether or not that youth would be fit and able, when the time came to take over the reins of leadership. We are building for the future, for the future of the British Race; for a future with fitness in mind, body and spirit is the attainable ideal for every man, woman and child in the country.[1]

With the aim of achieving the best fitness levels possible for young teenagers the National Youth Service Corps was formed, and by the end of 1941 at least forty areas had established a branch. The movement continued to gain strength and the long-term health of the nation's children began to dominate both government and public discourse. Monitoring health and providing adequate welfare provision initially presented some difficulties however. Pre-war health surveys relied on school medical inspections, but the Board of Education had suspended routine medical and dental inspections in 1939. City children would have slipped through the net in this respect in 1939 since their schools were closed. But those who were evacuated to the country were accused of infecting the countryside with head lice and scabies, despite the fact that existing medical records show a prevalence of such conditions in country areas prior to evacuation. Much of the problem stemmed from the futile use of commercially produced potions that claimed in strongly worded advertisements to eradicate lice, when they did nothing of the sort. The director of medical entomology, Professor Patrick Buxton of the London School of Hygiene and Tropical Medicine, eventually condemned the use of such potions in the public press and district nurses were given appropriate lotions to dispatch to schools and local communities. Moreover, as the war progressed and city schools reopened, detailed medical inspections were reinstated to monitor children's diets and child development. With a proportion of children migrating between city and country areas, these inspections tended to focus on camp schools in the country and inner-city schools where the child population remained relatively stable.

Generally speaking, many children were benefiting considerably from the medical discoveries and treatments that had been made throughout the 1930s and were being implemented on a wider scale during the war. For instance, parliamentary debates record several successes in terms of treating childhood diabetes thanks to medical scientists Banting and Best, and their discovery of insulin and its effects. Various new treatments were also introduced to combat simple and pernicious anaemia. Wider screening programmes were introduced for venereal diseases that affected children even before they were born, and health education prompted early diagnosis of congenital health problems. Indeed, in 1942, Mr R. McNair Wilson published a whole series of books including a text entitled *British Medicine*. In it he analysed and praised the research work of English doctors and scientists above all other nationalities, claiming that 'The English, contrary to general belief, are the scientific-minded of all peoples and so careful and exact with their observations that medical progress owes more to them than to any other race of mankind.'[2]

He went on to provide several fine examples of scientific endeavour in his extensive analysis, all of which supported his claim, though arguably the most important discovery of all – penicillin – was not included in his text. The enormous impact of this drug was felt in the armed forces during the war, but it was not readily available to the civilian population. Penicillin did not, therefore, make an impact on child health until after the war, when, in addition to its life-saving effects in aiding recovery from bacterial infections, it successfully combated venereal disease; thereby reducing the number of babies who were born deaf, blind or with other abnormalities as a result of their infected parents. Indeed, its eventual influence changed medical practice forever, since without antibiotics transplant surgery and a whole host of other surgical procedures would simply not be possible.

The greatest shift in health care policy towards children prior to the introduction of antibiotics was undoubtedly the focus on positive health measures. With regard to maintaining health and welfare for younger children, the wartime chief medical officer at the Ministry of Health, Sir Wilson Jameson, did much to inform the general public of the importance of good health and how to achieve it. Maternal and child health were placed top of his agenda, and he, like many of his colleagues, worked to achieve an overall improvement in these and other areas. His view reflected the majority of other ministers in the House of Commons who argued forcefully that child health was the most important element of the state; children would be the post-war future on which British society and industry would depend. 'We should consider that every young child should not be in so-called normal health but should have excellent health, with rosy cheeks, and should be romping round and asking questions in a way we always associate with a healthy child.'[3]

Health and Welfare

By 1942, officials at Whitehall were considering the prospect of post-war reconstruction. It can be argued that the foundations of the National Health Service were established from this point onwards. However, as some ministers, such as Dr Russell Thomas MP for Southampton, pointed out, the focus for attention seemed to be on curing ill health rather than maintaining good health. During a discussion on the Supply Committee report he called for a change of direction:

I always feel that in these debates we indulge in a form of dialectic materialism and do not actually discuss health at all. We incline to debate ill health the whole time. People speak as if they had a vested interest in disease instead of regarding health as an inheritance natural to us all. Nearly all children are born healthy. There are exceptions. Some have congenital disease and some are perhaps deficient, but, on the whole, they are born completely and absolutely healthy. Even the children of undernourished mothers come into the world healthy and strong at the expense of their mothers. I know it from experience. I think the Minister [of Health] should use that as his foundation of his view of the national health. Health is, and will be, maintained if there is sound nourishment, good housing and working conditions, and healthy exercise.[4]

As Dr Thomas further explained, children would be expected to rebuild Britain after the war and since national ill health was currently costing the country £300 million it made sense to apportion money to enhance the state of national health.[5] He also painted a bleak picture of the average working-class city mother:

When we come to the woman, the real head of the family, the story is often desperate. We all know how the buxom young woman starts out in life, full of hope, happy with her husband, and how they look forward to building their home. They look forward to their first child with joy. The second child comes and then the third. Her daily work mounts up, and there is more washing, more mending and less food to go round. A fourth and fifth child arrive and she is drained of her lime and iron. The buxom young woman becomes lean, stringy and bad tempered – the only unpaid worker in the country. At last she is unable to control her family, the house becomes desolate, she is unable to prepare proper meals – incidentally too many of our young women are unable to cook as they should – she is unable to cope with the situation, and her husband in despair at the discomfort, finds his way to the street corner with his single sixpence and puts it on the dogs in the hopes that he will become rich quick and end his misery.[6]

The view of Dr Thomas was echoed by many, and it was generally recognised within the corridors of power that the austere life of the majority of mothers needed to be improved in order to improve the lives of their children. Nevertheless, there was a considerable difference of opinion on how this improvement should be attained. The discourse tended to revolve around the issue of whether or not working-class mothers, in particular, were capable of raising their children properly. Child poverty was viewed by many as the result of financial mismanagement on the part of working-class mothers, and childhood illnesses the result of poor hygiene standards in working-class homes. Yet it was well known amongst working-class communities that every housewife took great pride in maintaining the cleanliness of her home. Even the door steps in front of their houses were scrubbed until they gleamed. Discipline in most families was also an important issue, since virtually every mother wanted her children to behave in an acceptable manner. Parental neglect and mistreatment of children was the exception rather than the norm. Even in families where fathers were away in the fighting forces grandfathers often stepped in to offer a guiding hand on the parental discipline front, and grandmothers stepped into the brink when mothers were working in the factories.

An extensive report by Sir William (later Lord) Beveridge published in 1942 proved conclusively that the root causes of poverty did not originate with working-class financial mismanagement. Nor did it stem from poor parental care, as parents often went without to give their children what they needed. Beveridge believed that since many families could not even afford to attend a doctor's surgery when they were ill, some form of social security was needed to cover individuals from the cradle to the grave. He acknowledged that cash handouts to the poor and sick were necessary in some instances, but they represented a fraction of a much broader problem. In terms of post-war reconstruction he identified what became known as the five giants that needed to be slain on the road to reconstruction. These were: want, disease, ignorance, squalor and idleness.[7]

Beveridge outlined a series of social security policies that were designed to initiate widespread welfare reform. These were formulated to encourage full employment, on which the whole scheme relied. In addition, he advocated the National Health Service, family allowances and the National Insurance Scheme. Such was the public interest in these radical new proposals that on the day of the report's publication there were queues over a mile long as people tried to get their hands on a copy. Thousands of copies were also flown and dropped to British servicemen overseas to encourage them to fight for a better post-war future. Beveridge's colleagues at Whitehall were not entirely convinced of his research findings, nor were they totally enamoured by his proposed scheme, but it was possible to detect some murmurings of support. Whereas earlier in the war ministers were concerned with child health and fitness in order to fight the war against Germany, by 1942 the situation had changed and Britain was no longer isolated. When Germany invaded Russia in June 1941 the latter joined forces with Britain; on 7 December the same year the Japanese attacked Pearl Harbor and the United States of America entered the war on Britain's side. British victories in North Africa in 1942 also prompted a tidal wave of public optimism. Suddenly it was not a matter of whether or not Britain would win the war, but when. Ministers could therefore envisage post-war reconstruction with a certain degree of confidence. Child health and welfare could now be viewed in terms of building a prosperous future for the British people. Beveridge was thus able to sell his report and recommendations to his critics on economic grounds. He did not, however, manage to completely change the notion that working-class mothers were primarily responsible for child poverty and ill health.[8] All the evidence nonetheless demonstrated that it was almost impossible for working-class families to escape the poverty trap.

With post-war reconstruction in mind, child health and welfare issues began to take centre stage at Whitehall. Naturally enough these issues began with the health of expectant mothers. The Technical Commission of the League of Nations had laid down firm guidelines for the minimum daily diet for expectant mothers as follows: 0.25lb meat, 8.5oz potatoes, 3.5oz green vegetables, 0.5oz root vegetables, 2pt milk, 1 egg, 1oz cheese and 1 spoonful each of cod liver oil, sugar and raw fruit.[9]

Wartime rationing did not allow for such an extravagant daily diet for British mums-to-be, but extra milk was available and radio doctors encouraged pregnant women to be creative with food. It was also possible for some mums to obtain extra meat on the black market. Though women who knowingly obtained black market goods were often ostracised by their communities. Stark government directives took great pains to point out the disloyalty of such women and praised the thrifty housewives. The following poem illustrates their view:

> The woman who wouldn't said, 'I have a pretty good time on the sly. It's easy to cheat with light petrol and heat. As for savings or work – I don't try.'
> The woman who wouldn't said, 'Queues are terribly hard on the shoes. But black market shopping is not. There's no stopping me shopping wherever I choose.'
> The woman who wouldn't said, 'Who is smarter than I? – not YOU. Wasting time stopping waste, Why I couldn't be faced with such wasteful distasteful to do.'
> But all thanks to the women like You. To the millions who would and who DO. Not selfishly spending but saving and mending and working to see Britain through.[10]

Ministry of Health officials focussed most of their attention on babies and infants under the age of 5. Guidelines for the care and feeding of these children were published from 1940 onwards, and the number of welfare officers increased. A proliferation of wartime nurseries also embraced the under-5s to allow women to enter into munitions factories to help with the war effort. The marriage bar was lifted in most working environments and government policy supported the working mother as far as possible. With so many young men away in the fighting forces the general demographic trend indicated a fall in the birth rate in rural areas during the war, but survival rates for babies increased. It was not government policy to compel mothers of young children under the age of 5 to undertake employment, but many wished to do so out of a sense of patriotic duty and in order to subsidise the family income.

Nevertheless, there was some dispute as to whether or not city wartime nurseries were beneficial to children. Criticisms abounded of city children placed in unsuitable nursery accommodation with very little to do and no constructive framework for play or learning. Welfare officials were also concerned that 2–5-year-olds were being placed alongside babies in wartime nurseries, where staff did not seem to have any training in childcare. But in many respects this was understandable; city nurseries had been established rapidly in response to a desperate need and no major planning or forethought was evident in their frameworks, other than an acknowledgement that these children needed to be fed and toileted. Questions raised in the House of Commons therefore focussed on these issues and attempted to make a distinction between wartime nurseries and nursery schools. Mr Messer, MP for Tottenham South, asserted:

> It seems to me that one is attempting to make capital out of a very difficult set of conditions in comparing war-time nurseries with nursery schools. When you are dealing with nursery schools, obviously the purpose is to deal with the children. War-time nurseries are not, objectively, to deal with the children, but with the parents. You want the parent to go into a munitions factory; the parent cannot unless you make some provision, and so you make what provision is possible. If there is criticism of the use of an Army hut for a nursery, in view of the fact that it is difficult to get anything at all, one has to accept it ... It should not be allowed to get abroad that the children of munitions workers are not being as well treated as they possibly can be in our war-time nurseries.[11]

Undoubtedly, city nurseries established for munitions workers were in some areas substandard when compared to organised pre-existing nursery schools. Most of the former were run by untrained staff, many of whom were volunteers. A large number of these staff had not even worked with children prior to their employment in the wartime nurseries. Thus city nursery children were often left to their own devices for long periods during the day. Many spent the whole day staring through the bars of their cots with only a few toys to occupy them. These same children, along with school-aged city children, nonetheless provided the focus for the bulk of official child health and welfare examinations. Height and weight measurements in particular yielded some interesting results.

Early wartime studies had indicated that children with parents of professional backgrounds fared better in terms of their overall health than those with working-class parents. This was not entirely surprising given the varying degrees in income levels. Sir John Orr conducted an experiment at Christ's Hospital public school and discovered that at the age of 13, boys at Christ's Hospital were 2.4in taller than boys of 13 in elementary schools. Boys of 17 at Christ's Hospital were 3.8in taller than boys of 17 in industry. Further experiments were conducted by increasing milk allowances, which proved that on average, children receiving free school milk grew 0.75in taller per year than their peers who did not receive extra milk.[12] Height measurements were not necessarily a firm indicator of health, but they did show that good quality nutrition made a significant and proven contribution to child growth and development rates.

Logically, therefore, ministers were eager to measure the height and weights of wartime children for whom nutrition had substantially improved throughout the war. These nutritional improvements were expected to bear fruit in terms of improved overall child development rates. Ministers awaited the outcome of child welfare investigations with bated breath. At one stage their impatience prompted the president of the Board of Education, Mr R.A. Butler, to point out with a hint of sarcasm that, 'it takes a little time for children to grow.'[13]

Once the long-awaited child development reports began to filter through to the ministers there was a sense of shock, confusion and, in some cases, total bewilderment. For one thing, children who were growing up in the cities surrounded by bombs and devastation appeared to be developing at much quicker rates than their counterparts in the country. They also appeared to be much healthier. Medical investigations had concentrated on city children and compared them with children who had been evacuated to camp schools in the country. The latter group received good diets and plenty of fresh air and exercise, but contrary to every expectation the health reports revealed that child growth rates were actually impaired in camp schools rather than improved.[14]

Ministers were deeply perplexed and some highly amusing ideas were bandied around the corridors of power as they tried to explain such profound anomalies. Whatever way they were approached, the child health reports simply did not make any sense. Some officials suggested that perhaps the children who attended the camp schools were subjected to too much exercise. Whilst others argued that the children may have had retarded growth rates to begin with and were simply unable to catch up at the same rate as city children. The director of the National Camps Corporation expressed his confusion over the statistics in a letter to N. Bosworth Smith of the Board of Education:

> I have read the report through several times and on each reading find it even more bewildering. It is small wonder that Dr Underwood finds it a 'little disconcerting' as the inference of the inquiry, as far as it has gone at present, would appear that it is better for a child to stay in East London sleeping irregular hours in ill ventilated shelters and eating fish and chips than to have fresh air conditions in one of our camps with regular hours of sleep and plenty of well prepared wholesome food (in which vegetables fresh from the garden play a large part) forming a diet balanced in accordance with the best advice obtainable from the Board of Education and others.[15]

Even more disconcerting for health ministers was the later evidence that trickled through Whitehall, which indicated that city children in areas such as London, Bristol, Birmingham and Sheffield actually had higher than average growth rates. Children were simply not developing as expected. In areas where good development was anticipated children were failing to thrive and in areas of destruction and catastrophe they were bursting with good health! Officials were naturally mystified. However, statistical evidence did eventually reveal that government efforts to improve overall child health had borne fruit. Children may not have gained height and weight in the manner predicted by Whitehall, nor in the geographical areas they expected, but they did achieve a level of health that surpassed pre-war years. There were fewer cases of childhood diseases such as measles and scarlet fever, fewer deaths from diphtheria and a greater resistance to infection generally. Fortunately, enemy bombing of sewers and water mains did not result in any waterborne diseases such as typhoid. Moreover, contrary to all expectations, city children thrived amongst the rubble. There was no question that better access to milk and food had brought about substantial health improvements.

Subsequently, within the corridors of power, ministers from all political parties reached an uneasy consensus about the need for some form of universal state welfare. As one MP, a Mr Davies, stated in the House of Commons in

June 1942: 'The health of a man or woman should not depend on the accident of geography – that because they happen to be in one place they shall get treatment denied to them in another place.'[16]

In addition to the recognition for the need for increased fairness in terms of health care delivery across Britain, there was also a sense of optimism about the level of health that could eventually be achieved for children and adults. Sir F. Fremantle asserted:

It is marvellous how the health of the nation has kept up in the war. This should mean better health after the war. If we make use of the experience of this war it should be, as the hon. member for Llanelly Mr J. Griffiths suggested, the basis of a great improvement in health after the war. War mixes up all classes of people and as it does that it opens the eyes of many of us to the possibilities of action and experience to which we were blind. War brings new ideas, new methods and new apparatus, and a good many of those things will help us after the war. When we say that however, let us also beware of complacency.[17]

There is no doubt that this spirit of optimism in the field of health was contagious and gave substantial impetus to the long-awaited and much appreciated National Health Service.

Notes

1   Parker, S.J., 'Youth Service Corps' in *Journal of Education*, vol. LXXVII, no. 1982, 14 March 1941, p. 209.
2   Hansard House of Commons Parliamentary Debates, 5th Series, 30 June 1942, vol. 385, col. 58.
3   Ibid., col. 124.
4   Ibid., col. 122.
5   Ibid., col. 125.
6   Ibid.
7   Lowe, R., *The Welfare State in Britain Since 1945* (1993), p. 126.

8   For a comprehensive analysis of the Beveridge Report, its critics and its shortcomings, please see Lowe, R., *The Welfare State in Britain Since 1945* (1993), pp. 125–35.

9   Hansard House of Commons Parliamentary Debates, 5th Series, 30 June 1942, vol. 385, col. 125.

10 HM Government Directive Report to the Women of Britain, Number 12, 1941.

11 Hansard House of Commons Parliamentary Debates, 5th Series, 30 June 1942, vol. 385, col. 85–86.

12 Ibid., col. 124.

13 Ibid., 11 December 1941, col. 1665.

14 National Archive PRO/ED/50/211.

15 Howarth to Bosworth Smith, 13 August 1942, National Archive PRO/ED/211.

16 Hansard House of Commons Parliamentary Debates, 5th Series, 30 June 1942, vol. 385, col. 86.

17 Ibid., col. 94.

7

Food, Glorious Food

At a time when food was in short supply because of shipping losses and the problems of importing foodstuffs from other countries, the British government did remarkably well in terms of feeding the nation. Indeed, it has since been acknowledged that the British diet was healthier during the war than at any other time in history. Furthermore, the Ministry of Health and the Ministry of Food made a formidable and successful team in terms of maintaining nutritional standards against severe and at times seemingly insurmountable odds. From the outset, babies, children and expectant mothers were given priority when food allowances were discussed and rationing was introduced.

Nutrition was considered to be a relatively new science and it was rightly regarded as being of the utmost importance to the health of the nation, especially when certain foods were unobtainable. Pre-war research had already determined the strong and indisputable link between poor diets and poor health. Experiments with monkeys, for instance, had revealed that they developed colitis and gastritis when fed on the same diets as those people living in poverty-stricken areas. It was also estimated that around 12 per cent of the insured population suffered from these afflictions and that much of the nation's ill health could be prevented by improved nutritional standards.[1]

Research had also revealed that the daily intake of foodstuffs in the poorest of families was deficient in virtually all vitamins. Perhaps rather surprisingly, with regard to child poverty research identified that the problem was not restricted to geographical areas in the north. Moreover, levels of poverty or affluence did not necessarily bare any relation to standards of nutrition. Whereas 25 per cent of children on Merseyside were living below the poverty line, a doctor in West Sussex discovered that 72 per cent of children were living below the nutritional standards laid down by the Children's Minimum Council.[2] In 1939 nutrition became a priority. Since no one knew how long the war would continue; it was important to keep the nation healthy; in part to maintain the essential war effort on the industrial and agricultural home front, but also to ensure that potential recruits into the armed forces were as fit as possible. This could only be done by ensuring that food was properly and fairly distributed throughout the land.

With this aim in mind, the Ministry for Food was established and basic food rations were introduced in January 1940. Lord Woolton was appointed the Minister of Food and, following advice obtained from the science division within the ministry, he duly formulated a national food policy. He stressed that, 'Milk and food distribution needed to be improved to maintain an efficient war effort and preserve the British race.'[3]

Rationing amounts tended to fluctuate slightly depending on availability, but generally rations per adult were as follows:

Bacon, ham or meat 4oz (100g) to the value of 1s 2d (roughly 6p today) weekly. Sausages were not rationed but difficult to obtain; offal was originally unrationed but sometimes formed part of the meat ration.
Butter 2oz (50g) weekly.
Cheese 2oz (50g), sometimes this rose to 4oz (100g) and even up to 8oz (200g) weekly.
Margarine or cooking fat 4oz (100g) weekly.
Milk 3pt (1800ml), sometimes dropping to 2pt (1200ml), weekly; in addition one packet of household skimmed and dried milk was available every month.
Sugar 8oz (200g) weekly.
Preserves 1lb (450g) every two months.
Tea 2oz (50g) weekly.
Eggs, 1 egg a week if available but at times dropping to 1 every two weeks. Dried egg powder was available and restricted to 1 packet a month.
Sweets 12oz (350g) every month.

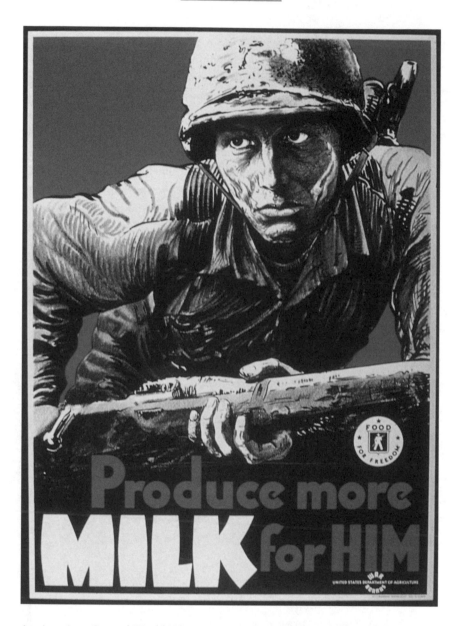

An American Second World War poster promoting milk, 1941–45. (US National Archives and Records Administration/Wikimedia Commons)

There was also a monthly points system that allowed a person to buy 1 can of fish or meat, 2lb (0.9kg) of dried fruit or 8lb (3.6kg) of split peas. Babies and younger children, and expectant and nursing mothers, had orange juice and cod liver oil from welfare clinics together with priority milk. This milk was also available to invalids.[4] Every adult was issued with a ration book, and children's ration books were issued to mothers. Tea coupons were not cut out of children's ration books however – instead of tea they were used to buy oranges when available.

Rationing was not popular with the general public and the choice of available food was limited, but it did mean that thousands of families enjoyed a far higher standard of nutrition because their purchasing power was restricted to foods of guaranteed nutritional value. The Ministry of Food, alongside the Ministry of Health, laid down cooking and shopping guidelines for all housewives, and were especially attentive to mothers with young children, issuing golden rules for feeding children as follows:

Give the children their full body building rations, milk, cheese, eggs,
    bacon and meat
Give salads and vegetables at the beginning of the meal while the child's
    appetite is still keen.
Avoid fried foods. They are seldom digested.
Don't let the children have too much starchy food – bread, cereals,
    puddings, etc. Give these after they've had their body building foods.
Don't let the children have pepper, mustard or vinegar.[5]

In a concerted national effort to improve children's nutrition, in July 1941 central government went one step further and offered financial incentives to local authorities to extend the school meals service. This move was intended to relieve the burden on host families who were taking in evacuees, and to relieve the burden on the many mothers who were working long hours in munitions factories and other war work. The latter were often too exhausted to contemplate cooking a large meal after a long day's labour.

By the end of August 1941, 110 new communal feeding centres had sprung up around the country, and it was made illegal to charge more than 5*s* for a meal. Nevertheless, some of these feeding centres were the result of voluntary endeavour rather than local authority initiatives. Although it was made compulsory for factories to provide canteens and eventually 2,000 British restaurants were established in cities across the country. Radio doctors were also apt to put out the benefits of cold food, initially to justify the lack of facilities in reception areas, and later on to encourage those who had been bombed out of their homes to eat raw foodstuffs. Eating cold food also saved the nation's fuel.

You have heard perhaps of the Oslo breakfast. This is a cold meal full of vitamins. In Norway it consists of milk, a kind of wholemeal bread, margarine or butter, goats cheese and half an apple, half an orange or a raw carrot. They found that children who started the day with this breakfast flourished. The London County Council have been trying it, not as breakfast but as a dinner. This was given to a number of children and their progress compared with that of others on the good old-fashioned hot dinner. For every inch that a 'hot dinner child' grew, the 'Oslo child' grew 1.75in, and 2in in the case of a girl. In weight the 'Oslo boy' put on twice as much as the 'hot dinner boy'. 'Oslo children' were healthier, with fewer ailments and much better complexions.[6]

Councils were indeed encouraging food comparison programmes with regard to children, particularly in those of school age. But early dietary programmes, in terms of measuring food intake and the height and weight of children, were inconclusive, since there were many variables to consider and most council members did not adopt rigorous research methods. No account was taken of possible hormonal changes for instance, or more importantly what the children ate when they got home.

Furthermore, schools were experiencing severe problems, especially those in the cities, with many of them still closed. Other schools were finding it difficult to obtain suitable premises to convert into dining rooms. Therefore a countrywide extension of the school meals system did not really get under way until the end of 1941. The scheme was spearheaded and given impetus however, by the success that Anglesey had achieved in implementing the service. Anglesey had provided 60 per cent of its schools with meals by June 1942 and was intent on ensuring that all schools would receive meals by the end of that year. Addressing the House of Commons in 1942 the MP Mr R.A. Butler proclaimed:

> Over 700,000 children are now taking midday meals at school. Last year
> 1,733 proposals providing for 240,000 children were approved, and from

January to May of this year an increased number covering some quarter million children have been sanctioned. I see no reason why the target already mentioned, of 1,000,000 meals a day for children should not be reached by the end of the summer. The outstanding success comes from Anglesey. The Director of Education whose views I quote because they exactly represent what we at the Board feel, calls attention to the almost incredible effect of the provision of school meals on the health of the children as reflected in their wellbeing, their zest for life and their alertness. I can bear that out from our experience all over the country, wherever this system of school meals has been started. I trust this remarkable lead will be followed, not only in Wales but also in England.[7]

The school meal service did indeed expand substantially, and while a few schools continued to have problems with premises, the overall trend was one of rapid improvement. Whereas only one child in thirty was fed at school in 1940, by 1945 this figure was one in three.[8] Undoubtedly the school meals service had an enormous impact on the lives of children and although the quality of food varied from area to area, the standard was generally good. Children still had to surrender their meat rations to school canteens despite objections to this policy from the director of education. Lord Woolton had acknowledged the difficulties that would be associated with running a school meals service with coupons, but had also decided that any exception in favour of school canteens and communal feeding centres would undermine the principles of rationing. Great care was taken to ensure the nutritional content of school meals and a number of teachers reported that many children had never even seen a lettuce until the service was introduced. To the chagrin of government ministers, however, as they renewed their pleas for mothers to send their children out of the cities, there was still no evidence – nutritionally or otherwise   that children were happier or healthier in the country. A memo from the Board of Education to school inspectors in country areas had suggested a different approach might persuade city mothers to part with their children:

What we should like to have is not a report of a formal of statistical nature but rather the kind of 'story' which reveals the spirit of the children, teachers, foster parents and so on, and which illustrates some of the social and educational effects of bringing children from towns and into different surroundings.[9]

Propaganda aimed at persuading city mothers to part with their children tended to fall on deaf ears. Indeed, enemy action had more of an effect on city mothers than government persuasion did. By 1941 the problem was not simply a matter of the emotional attachment to their children; economic considerations also dictated their decisions. As the war progressed inflation rocketed and city mothers, especially those with several children, could not afford to pay the billeting allowances that were required by host families in the countryside. They also needed the children's ration books to contribute to healthy family meals, and these would need to be surrendered to host families if they sent their children out of the cities. Contrary to popular belief, therefore, the majority of children continued to remain in cities. Family economics and the need for as many ration coupons as possible had in part superseded parental emotions.

In an effort to improve nutritional education the BBC broadcast twice-weekly programmes named *The Kitchen Front*. Marguerite Patten OBE was in charge of the Ministry of Food Advice Bureau at Harrods and was a regular contributor to the programme. She recalled that:

> Many of the ingredients available, such as dried egg and wartime national flour, were a challenge to any cook, but it was surprising how we learned to cope with these and produce edible dishes. Virtually every cook in Britain behaved like a zealous squirrel – we bottled and or dried fresh fruits; we salted beans; we prepared economical chutneys and pickles; we made the best of every available ingredient. We ate lots of vegetables and home produced fruits but little fat, sugar or meat. Our menus may have been monotonous, but both adults and children were incredibly healthy and we all felt that we were playing a vital role towards the ultimate victory when we could all happily look forward to eating much more varied and exciting dishes once again.[10]

To encourage children to learn the value of food bedtime stories were told that incorporated the essential messages for children. The following are just three examples of such rhymes:

The Queen of Hearts

The Queen of Hearts
Said 'No' to tarts
'There's wheat-meal bread for tea.
Each cream-gold slice
Is Oh so nice.
And better far for me.'[11]

The Song of Potato Pete

Potatoes new, potatoes old
Potato in a salad cold
Potatoes baked or mashed or fried
Potatoes whole, potato pied
Enjoy them all, including chips,
Remembering spuds don't come in ships.[12]

Bedtime Story

Once upon a time there were five housewives.
There names were Lady Peel potatoes
The Hon. Mrs Waste fuel,
Miss Pour the vegetable water down the sink,
Mrs Don't like uncooked vegetables and
Mrs Won't eat carrots.
Don't let one of them put a nose in your kitchen.[13]

Children were taught about vitamins and the importance of eating the correct food at school too. Radio doctors hammered home the message to mothers and legislation was introduced that made it an offence to waste food. Raw vegetables were recommended wherever possible, especially cress, chicory, endives, carrots, cabbage, beetroot and dandelion leaves. As the radio doctor proclaimed, these products needed to be known as 'all things raw and beautiful'. Lectures were also given by dieticians in various public places. as one woman recorded in her diary:

Miss Andross, a dietician of the Dough School, had arranged an exhibition of wartime foods. We saw a loaf baked with potato flour, a substitute for wheaten flour that they seem anxious to introduce. This loaf smelt very nice but it does not seem popular. Potato flour is more likely to make its hit in scones. Several platefuls of scones were displayed with various substitutes for wheaten flour – barley, rye, oats, potato, chocolate potato, and 'black bread' which is a mixture of rye, oats and barley. There were two dishes displayed as contrasts, one was macaroni cheese, accompanied by a piece of plain bread, it being impossible to spread the butter; the other was meant to do without bread and butter as an accompaniment, so that you now would not need the plain bread. I think it was macaroni cheese with potato added, but I got a little mixed. Miss Andross has made preparations from most wild fruits (sloe conserve, wild raspberry jam, crab apple jelly etc.) and had a soup made from pulped rosehips, which was supposed to be highly nutritious and very tasty. There were bottles containing all sorts of vegetables preserved in brine; there were dried vegetables to be soaked in water, and dried mint and dried parsley chopped small; also French beans preserved by being buried in a jar of salt. I just came home in time to hear the Archbishop of York on 'justice'. He puts so much into fifteen minutes that you can't retain it all.[14]

Advice from all quarters stressed the importance of eating some raw green vegetables every single day. Iris Williams recalled the dedication and effort that was put into normal everyday food planning and religious festivals such as Christmas:

I used to get a rolling pin out and crush the saccharin to make the sugar go further. At Christmas we had monkey nuts and a tangerine in the toe of our stockings but no oranges or bananas or anything like that. Zoning of food was restricted to the area where it was grown because of transport problems. We had onion gravy instead of liver and onions and we queued for hours to get an extra bit of offal.[15]

There were treats of course, for special celebrations like children's birthdays. Blancmange powder was often mixed with condensed or dried milk and jelly was also popular on these occasions. Cakes were baked whenever ingredients allowed, although often without eggs, and the jam filling was frequently made from carrots or swedes. To make up for the lack of sweets and desserts, parties focussed on providing children with a wide variety of games. They were also encouraged to dress up as characters from nursery rhymes or history in much the same way as today. Out of necessity wartime parties focussed on fun rather than food.

Surprisingly, early health reports suggested that city children appeared to fare better than their country counterparts on the food front. In view of the fact that most food was grown in the countryside, these reports seemed to present a strange anomaly. However, the organisation of food distribution was far more efficient in cities, and the majority of families had adopted a policy of bringing elements of the countryside into their city homes. For instance, it became popular for city families to keep chickens in their backyard. This allowed them to obtain extra eggs and a chicken now and then for supper. One the most overriding memories for city children living in the old two-up two-down houses was not just the bombs, but the frantic run to the outside toilet. These children frequently went out to their backyards to use the toilet in bare feet and needed to run very quickly across the yard to avoid the chickens pecking at their feet. Rabbits were also kept in city yards to provide a rabbit stew when meat rations were scarce, though many were reprieved and saved from the stewing pot by a child's protesting tears. Every piece of available land was used to plant vegetables and city children became adept at learning how to make compost heaps and grow food. Incidentally, the dietary dependence on vegetables, particularly potatoes, rather than wheat products, resulted in the almost accidental discovery of celiac disease. Paediatricians began to notice an improvement in the health of babies and children who had previously been suffering from intestinal problems when they ate more vegetables and no bread. These children were subsequently found to be suffering from gluten intolerance.

As the war progressed milk played an increasingly important role in child nutrition as a valuable source of protein. City children were again fortunate in that milk distribution was also more efficient for them. A number of rural areas and small towns experienced problems with dairy departments in their boroughs. A few, like Kettering, experienced a shortage of glass bottles and their dairy department was unable to provide the usual 0.33pt bottles in sufficient numbers. Teachers in these areas refused to accept bulk milk deliveries and supply was subsequently suspended.[16] Furthermore, milk supplied to country areas was often of dubious quality since very few small dairies had treatment plants. As previously noted, this problem resulted in the alarming rise in childhood bovine tuberculosis in the countryside and highlighted the importance of the pasteurisation process.

In contrast, city children were supplied with pasteurised milk by larger national dairies and thus escaped the perils of drinking untreated milk. This division between those children drinking untreated milk and those drinking safe milk became more pronounced after 1941 when meat rations to school canteens were cut due to supply problems. Milk rations were increased to compensate for the reduction in meat rations and the government outlined a target for 100 per cent milk consumption in schools. The cases of tuberculosis in children living in the countryside soared rapidly as a result. Central government could not be held totally responsible for the actions of individual local authorities however, who almost certainly knew the risk they were taking with children's health by not bringing local milk producers into line with central government recommendations. This situation, perhaps more than any other, illustrated how easily government intentions could be thwarted by local authorities. On the whole, national food policy and rationing was an undoubted success.

Indeed, the combined efforts of the Ministries of Health and Food to provide a fair and sound food policy, gained great respect from fellow ministers. Captain Elliston, praising these efforts in Parliament in 1942, pointed out:

> It is quite remarkable, in spite of our shipping troubles and loss of supplies from all quarters of the world, that we have been able to maintain a diet for the people, which apparently is maintaining their health and strength. One realises, of course, that great vigilance is required, and one is glad to know that in this, the third year of the war there is no reason for any immediate anxiety. But the Ministry are rightly exercising great vigilance because none of us can tell what delayed effects may arise as a result of the changes and deprivations of diet we are now undergoing.[17]

The food industry also played a part in helping to relieve the monotony of food rationing. Cadburys, for instance, published a recipe booklet aimed at making the all-important treat rations go just that bit further. The booklet was published for 1*d* and raised money for the British Red Cross. Other companies came to the rescue of those huddled in shelters. J. Lyons of Cadby Hall provided and sold food at a reasonable price to the London Tube Refreshment Service. Food was delivered to depots at the end of each tube line, and tube refreshments were then taken by train to special service points on each platform. In the afternoon boilers were turned on in readiness, and each evening tea and cocoa was served to those taking refuge in one of the seventy-nine Underground tube stations, along with a variety of food. In terms of providing food in adverse conditions, the London Tube Refreshment Service was perhaps the most organised and consistent food distribution service ever to be provided during the Blitz.

The ways in which ordinary families managed to cope with food shortages was truly remarkable. Moreover, the visible and notable improvement in child nutrition during a time of severe conflict was nothing short of astonishing. But it was also important to monitor such a momentous change. As the Minister of Health stated categorically:

We are working in effective co-operation with the Ministry of Food and the President of the Board of Education, and we have put the babies and children first. We regard it as important to watch the food situation from the health point of view, and have made arrangements to secure accurate and prompt information to check the results of our joint work on standards of nutrition throughout the country. This work is carried out by Regional Medical Officers, The Emergency Hospital Service and by special local surveys. These surveys have been undertaken with the help and guidance of expert medical officers supplied by the International Health Division of the Rockefeller Foundation.[18]

All subsequent international and domestic surveys confirmed that dietary improvements had revitalised British children. Canadian doctors even published articles lauding the success of British government food policy towards children. All surveys suggested that children's energy levels had increased along with their resistance to disease, and educational tests in some schools revealed that attention to school work had also improved. Ministers were greatly relieved by the generally positive results of these investigations, but some of their conclusions were difficult to understand. Just as early health surveys had proved that camp schoolchildren in the countryside were failing to develop at the normal rate, these later surveys confirmed without any doubt that city children were thriving far better than country children. This one simple but glaring fact baffled both the science departments and nutritional experts at Westminster. Children, it seemed, were determined to defy all logic.

Notes

1   Hansard House of Commons Parliamentary Debates, 5th Series, 30 June 1942, vol. 385, col. 124.
2   Ibid., col. 123.
3   National Archive ED/50/215.
4   Patten. M., *The Victory Cook Book* (1995), p. 2.
5   Ibid., p. 15.
6   BBC Home Service radio broadcast, 22 November 1939, quoted in Garfield, S., *We Are At War* (2005), p. 71.
7   Hansard House of Commons Parliamentary Debates, 5th Series, 16 June 1942, vol. 385, col. 1407.
8   Titmuss, R., *Problems of Social Policy* (1950), p. 421.
9   National Archive ED/22/215, official memo to school inspectors, SN 645.
10   Patten. M., *The Victory Cook Book* (1995), p. 2–3.
11   Ibid., p.77.
12   Ibid., p.36.
13   Ibid., p.42.
14   Garfield, S., *We Are At War* (2005), p. 398–399.
15   Oral history testimony: Williams, Iris, 2011.
16   Sharp, P., 'How the Children lost their Milk' in *Journal of Education*, vol. LXXIV, no. 1928, 22 December 1939, p. 518.
17   Hansard House of Commons Parliamentary Debates, 5th Series, 30 June 1942, vol. 385, col. 143.
18   Ibid., col. 73.

8

Child Psychology

T he numerous and disturbing child development reports that fell like autumn leaves onto the desks of perplexed health ministers in Whitehall were like manna from heaven for child psychologists. They had been arguing vigorously, without any supporting evidence, for some years that a strong link existed between a child's emotional and psychological wellbeing and the ability of a child to develop normally. Major discrepancies in child height and weight measurements between city children and those who were evacuated to the country continued to baffle health ministers, but simultaneously added weight to these arguments and stressed the importance of child psychology. The child health reports also bucked the overall trend in terms of adult mental health, since one of the most astonishing facts relating to the Second World War pertains to the psychology of the adult British population as a whole. Despite the trauma of the Blitz and the deprivations caused by clothes and food rationing, the incidence of adult mental health problems actually dropped dramatically. Reporting to the Supply Committee in 1942 the MP Mr Brown announced this trend with some surprise:

At the beginning of the war it was feared – and feared by specialists – that the strain of war conditions, particularly under aerial bombardment, would lead to a serious increase of mental disorders. The contrary has proved to be the fact. In 1938 the number admitted to mental hospitals was 30,000, and it was the same in 1939. In 1940 it fell to 28,000, and in 1941 these are the years that covered the big bombings – to 26,000, that is, 4,000 fewer than in the years of peace. That seems to me to be an eloquent testimony of the nerves of the nation, and it should assure Hitler that his attempt to break the nerve of our people by the terror by night has failed. He will not fret the fibre of our resolution or break our nerve. I do not think that any prophet would have prophesised that our crowded populations would have stood the test of nerves so well.[1]

But while the nerves of the adult population were bearing up well, there were no accurate figures to discern whether the same could be said of the nation's children. In fact, child psychology, either as a discipline for investigation or as grounds for treatment, was decidedly lacking in most areas. Child welfare agencies concentrated on physical health and wellbeing, and no real thought had been given to the emotional or psychological needs of children. There was some limited recognition amongst parents, welfare officers and teachers that a few children were more sensitive than others but these observations were often not recorded, and it was generally believed that children would eventually grow out of their difficulties in this respect. There were even some who genuinely believed that children's minds were a blank canvas on which adults could merely imprint their own characteristics. Wartime observations of children, however, along with detailed records of their overall development, henceforth changed adult perceptions of childhood.

It would be wrong to assume that government officials paid no attention whatsoever to the minds of children; they may not have thought much about the emotional impact of evacuation schemes or the general circumstances of war, but they were nonetheless keen to shield them from political rhetoric and conscientious objectors. In fact, it was considered vital that older children in particular were not deterred from joining the armed forces and defending their country. Thus secondary schoolteachers who were known to be conscientious objectors were either dismissed from their posts or relocated into primary schools. In some respects this process could be viewed as an unfair measure, since most schoolteachers would not have inflicted their political views onto their pupils. However the policy was a natural precaution; Britain was fighting for its very existence and pacifism was liable to undermine the war effort on a fundamental level.

At the outbreak of war adults did their best to protect children from any talk of war, and during the phoney war period it was still possible to shield children to some extent from events that were taking place in Europe. Once the Blitz began it was a different story, especially for city children who were increasingly subjected to the realities of war on a nightly basis. Gradually city children became not only fully aware of the war, since it was on their doorstep, but also very much a part of the overall war effort. From fundraising efforts for the armed forces to helping out in factories, shops and within the domestic environment, these children formed an integral part of the community spirit engendered by the Blitz, and were no longer shielded from hostilities. Child welfare officials were naturally concerned by this trend, since most had expected the majority of children to be living in reception areas away from the bombing. Amongst these professionals there were a number who propounded alarmist theories and predictions, claiming that Britain would have to contend with a post-war generation of shell-shocked neurotic children because of the Blitz conditions. The pioneering work of psychoanalyst Anna Freud however, put paid to such outlandish and exaggerated predictions.

Anna Freud was the daughter of the famous psychoanalyst Sigmund Freud and she initiated her research into the psychological responses of children to war by comparing those children who stayed in the cities alongside those who had been evacuated and later returned. Anna Freud had fled to England with her father in 1936 following some intense and extremely unpleasant Nazi interrogations. A long-time devotee of her father's work, Anna had grown up surrounded by a variety of psychoanalytical theories. As such, she developed psychological theories of her own and was convinced that the key to normal mental health began with the development of adequate emotional and psychological skills in childhood. With this special interest in child psychology she founded the first psychoanalytical clinic for children in West Hampstead, London. The war gave Freud the perfect opportunity to conduct her research, which particularly focussed on childhood reactions to trauma and distress.

During the research process Freud discovered that certain defence mechanisms came into play during childhood that shielded the mind from excessive trauma. More importantly, she argued that these same defence mechanisms were then carried on into adulthood. Thus an adult would often revert to childhood behaviours when confronted with trauma. For instance, adult withdrawal, denial, aggression, suppression and fantasy could all be related to childhood mental defence strategies. Until this point no one had thought of examining the psychology of childhood. It was assumed by many that children merely adopted their parents' characteristics by a gradual process of mental transference. Compared with her father's theories, Anna's work differed somewhat by focussing more on the ego and how this developed in children.

With funds obtained from the American Foster Parents Plan, Freud established a wartime nursery with her best friend, Dorothy Burlingham. This nursery housed 120 infants ranging from six months–upwards. Freud ensured that siblings were kept together and structured them into family units for security and observation. She also encouraged firemen and rescue workers to act as male role models where none existed. Freud argued that the psychological effects of bombing were external anxieties for children and reassurance was all that was required to relieve them of their fear. Not all psychoanalysts agreed with this view however, and some, such as Melanie Klein, maintained that the war merely acted as a catalyst for internal psychological conflicts.

Eventually Anna Freud became widely acknowledged as the founder of child psychoanalysis, since she compiled the very first detailed records of child psychological developments. These records documented various child behavioural patterns in an attempt to demonstrate the normal from the abnormal; to measure the mental processes of maturity and changes that occurred in children as a result of war. Sleep patterns, eating habits, attention spans, memory recall, drawing and writing skills, knowledge retention, play behaviour and learning patterns were all recorded in depth.

Certain childhood behaviours were subsequently identified as problematic in terms of psychological development. Enuresis (bed-wetting), for instance, was defined as a mental protest, a way in which a child could demonstrate that something was amiss, since it was frequently a manifestation of unhappiness. Eating disorders were similarly an indication that there was a psychological trauma. Often, Freud discovered that certain behavioural changes highlighted the presence of a time lag in a child's psychological development. With meticulous observations and records Freud became adept at determining childhood psychological norms, against which she could diagnose and treat those children who were experiencing problems.

Furthermore, this new process of child psychoanalysis provided some startling insights into a child's world, and some rather curious discoveries. Indeed to many health care professionals Freud's research findings were surprising to say the least. In the process of observing and recording the ways in which children mentally coped with trauma and distress Freud discovered that city children who stayed with their mothers, fathers or grandparents were emotionally more stable and far happier than those who had been evacuated. While the latter suffered from homesickness, enuresis, depression, eating disorders and, in a few cases, suicidal tendencies, children who remained in cities seemed to thrive emotionally and develop a well-balanced approach to the bombing. Freud argued that not only were children not automatically afraid of air raids, in some children war actually gave vent to a child's natural aggressive instincts. Even those who admitted to being nervous and fearful also expressed excitement and a greater sense of family intimacy during the air raids.

Some indication of the lives of city children during air raids and the reactions of their mothers can be gleaned from individual diaries written for the Mass Observation surveys. The reactions of mothers naturally changed throughout the war, especially once the bombing began in earnest, but children seemed more resilient and adaptable, taking most events in their stride. A mother of three confided to her diary:

My children don't seem to be taking much notice of the war. The eldest boy has come home with various songs ridiculing Hitler and making fun of the ARP, such as 'Snow White made a shirt, Hitler wore it, Chamberlain tore it, Blimey what a shirt'. Sometimes the names are reversed so I don't know which is the correct version. Another is 'Underneath the Chestnut tree, Hitler dropped a bomb on me, now I'm a blinking refugee, Underneath etc.'[2]

A few weeks later the same mother revealed her own fears:

I feel that I must write in my diary regularly these days; things are happening so quickly and one feels that one has a seat in the front row of the stalls at the making of history. Sometimes I feel that we are coming to the very evening of civilisation, and that the noise and roar of battle are the last crashing chords of the finale. But my deeper conviction is that we shall come out in the end … if we can hold them now. If I don't feel nervous that the grim drama is going to come down and include me, although sometimes I suffer some apprehensions on the behalf of my children. I can so easily conjure up the hateful possibilities of myself and the children homeless, of the feeling of utter desolation that must come

Battersea incident, London, January 1945. A young girl stands among the ruins, British flag overhead. Corresponds to a V-2 rocket bombing on 27 January 1945: seventeen people killed, twenty houses destroyed, dozens more houses damaged. (Wikimedia Commons)

upon people in those circumstances, the loss of security and stability, and above all the terrible feeling of being unprotected. But that, let us hope, is only the playing of my imagination. I have thought that for the first time I have noticed some effects of the war on the general atmosphere of my children. Dick, aged eleven, is quietly excited, almost as a boy before a firework display. But Bobbie aged six, is getting rather strung up. Only Janet, the baby, remains calm and cheerfully smiling all the time.[3]

This mother's feelings of fear dissipated over time however, as she and her children grew accustomed to the bombing. Later entries in her diary demonstrate a new resolve and a more composed approach to the Blitz. There was even evidence to support the notion that people were becoming used to the adrenalin rush that accompanied bombing raids and thriving on the experience:

> While we were playing Monopoly, the kids were laughing and chattering, but I could hear thuds and explosions in the distance and I felt frightened underneath. For a moment everything seemed to lose its stability. But my fear wasn't unpleasant, it had a thrill like daring or something, and when the next day came with no further raids I found myself wishing for the warning sound so that I could feel we were getting on with the job. This morning Dick said to me, 'I feel bored now on days when there is no warning.'[4]

Attitudes to the enemy were also mixed. Manifestations of the finely tuned British sense of justice and decency could be detected in the fact that most people made a distinction between Hitler and his Nazis, and the ordinary German people, many of whom had resisted Nazi ideology and the regime's totalitarian state. Tilly Rice recorded her thoughts about the enemy's goal in her diary following a much-needed day trip into the country with her children:

> Today we had the car out for a drive and had a lovely afternoon cruising round: Guildford, Frensham Ponds, Devils Punchbowl, Milford, Newlands Corner, Box Hill – a good dose of Surrey's spacious and lovely vistas coming as a fine antidote to air raid nights. Looking out over those hills and planes, aeroplanes and bombs seemed something very small. And sitting after tea, alone on a sunlit veranda while the family went off to explore, comfortably smoking a cigarette, looking at the white cupola on top of the granary, I thought what a stupidly impossible task the Germans had taken on. To fight to Nazify Britain ... why, they'd have to destroy the whole country and start from the very soil up.[5]

Nevertheless, while adults had a clear idea of the enemy's ambitions, notions of war and feelings about the enemy were often confused in the minds of children. When Anna Freud published the results of her first wartime psychological survey in 1943 she revealed that children interpreted enemy action in a variety of ways. Whereas many took unpredictable events and bombing in their stride, others revealed a level of anxiety that resulted in regression, withdrawal or aggression. Quite a number of children also imbued the enemy with benevolent characteristics. For instance, one young girl named Janet decided that the Germans must be quite kind because they did not drop a bomb on her house while she was in the air-raid shelter.[6]

Freud discovered that even city children with bad or neglectful parents thrived better than those who had been forced by the process of evacuation to sever their parental connections. Official reports conducted by medical officers, social workers and school inspectors confirmed Freud's research findings. Without exception, these reports claimed that children in the throes of the Blitz were able to maintain an astonishing level of emotional stability, regardless of the bombing, providing they were able to remain with their parents or other close relatives. This was a rather curious revelation as one school medical officer who had travelled from city to city observed:

> I have had the opportunity to see several hundred children during the last month. On several occasions I saw them and watched them while bombs were falling in the neighbourhood and air raids were overhead and asked them questions relating to the war, sirens etc … Children have adapted themselves to their present conditions of life surprisingly well … Even children who were bombed out of their homes did not seem to suffer in any way … There is no question of shock.[7]

It is clear that city children did thrive against the odds, but much of their fear of the enemy and their thoughts about war were expressed in their school activities. By the time that Freud had published her first psychological survey the war had infiltrated the curriculum of most schools. Children were encouraged to bring in money for 'Salute the Soldier Week' and 'Wings for Victory Week' and were involved in knitting socks, balaclavas and other items for the armed forces. Children's art featured submarines, Spitfires and battle ships, and they always had the nation's defences in place. For example, teachers noted that regardless of whether children were painting landscapes or portraits, patterns or diagrams, they always included anti-aircraft guns and three or four barrage balloons in their artwork. A positive outlook was maintained at all times and national poster competitions encouraged children to paint pictures of the armed forces winning the war. In addition to their artwork, war began to influence their school playground games. Boys would tear around the playgrounds with their arms outstretched pretending to be war planes, whilst girls waited for them to land and pretended to nurse their injuries. When schools were bombed the only anxiety to be expressed by pupils was usually related to the survival of the tuck shop.

Ribald songs about the enemy that were sung in the air-raid shelters found their way to the playground, and children often told each other jokes about the enemy. Teachers noted however, that the words of some songs and jokes went over the heads of innocent children. For instance a popular song at the time contained the lines 'Hitler has only got one ball, the other is in the Albert Hall'; children interpreted this song as amusing because they thought it was silly of Hitler to want two footballs in the first place, and even sillier for him to keep one in the Albert Hall. Nevertheless, the process of ridiculing the enemy took away much of the fear and acted as a defence mechanism for both adults and children.

Children's literature also offered an opportunity to vent emotions and identify with characters who were taking part in wartime life. Children's authors and their publishers acknowledged the need to provide stories for children coping with the Blitz as well as those living in reception areas, and this was a clear indication that a large proportion of children had remained in cities. One of the most popular story series for children during this era centred on the *Just William* character, and was created by Richmal Crompton Lamburn. The 11-year-old playful schoolboy and prankster 'Just' William and his loyal friends, the 'outlaws', summed up children's confusion with regard to the complexity of the adult world and to war. The fictional series highlighted the values and restrictions encompassed within family life and society, alongside children's efforts to understand the ways of the world. Thus within the text Crompton portrays children as the perplexed observers of grown-ups and their actions. Often the story lines included a battle of wits between children and adults, in which the children were usually victorious.

The series was so popular that it was broadcast on the BBC. The following titles give some indication as to how William's adventures followed the course of the war: *William the Dictator* (1938), *William and the Air Raid Precautions* (1939), *William and the Evacuees* (1940), *William Does His Bit* (1941) and *William Carries On* (1941). All of these stories were designed to entertain children while simultaneously explaining to them some of the circumstances of war. In addition, they provided children with much-needed humour and emotional diversions from the more distressing aspects of war. Undoubtedly children were more resilient than had hitherto been recognised, but they were still prone to worrying about their own safety and that of their relations and friends.

Teachers very quickly adopted the policy of keeping children busy virtually every minute of the schoolday in order to keep them from brooding or worrying unduly about the prospect of air raids. When lessons were interrupted by such raids teachers generally referred to them as nuisance raids in an attempt to dismiss the potential threat and calm the children's fears. Many young children were not aware of the details of war but they did manage to construct a simplistic version of the threat to their home and country. A gentleman who was aged 6 when war broke out explained:

> We knew there was a war on. The only time we realised that it was very serious was when the teachers came in one afternoon and said we'd all got to pray because all of our soldiers were coming home from a place called Dunkirk, and we would have ten minutes prayer for them, to get them home safely. So we realised it was very serious then, because from the look on the teacher's face, you would have thought that Hitler was standing outside the classroom door waiting to take her away.[8]

Older children were obviously more aware of the events in Europe. Iris Williams was aged 12 when war broke out and recalled with some clarity the situation from a child's standpoint:

> I remember the silence in our home that followed the radio announcement by Neville Chamberlain telling us that Britain was at war with Germany. My father had enlisted in the army, in the Pioneer corps, and during his training my mother made sure that we went away to be near his training camps for weekends. We all spent some precious time together before he went away to war. I obviously absorbed everything from the Pathe news that was shown at the cinemas. I knew about the invasion of Poland

and the fall of France. I knew that Hitler was the baddie and he had lots of followers. My mother was very worried about the prospect of a German invasion because she had two girls, me and my sister who was six years younger. But I didn't think about the Germans much at all, I was a very shy girl and quite accepting of things generally. We just got on with our lives. Mum didn't want us to be evacuated and I certainly didn't want to leave her. I was quite a nervous child and I didn't like change. Mum did a cleaning job at some very nice houses and she would take us with her. The gardener at one of them used to give her bunches of dahlias to take home and some fruit. Then my mum used to cycle around collecting insurance premiums. My uncle used to pop in and see if we were alright because he worked for the aircraft industry and it was a reserved occupation. The local church minister also looked in on us and often stopped to chat to my mum. During the summer months we often slept in our Anderson shelter, which meant that we didn't have to make a dash from the house in the middle of the night when the sirens sounded the warning that enemy aircraft were approaching. In winter the shelters would flood after heavy rain and sumps were dug to drain off the water. But it was too cold to be in the shelters in winter unless absolutely necessary. Always the searchlights would be sweeping the sky at night and we would be woken by the anti-aircraft guns sometimes before the sirens. Often we didn't get much sleep at all but still had to get up and carry on as normal. One of the girls in our school form was killed when there was a direct hit on her family's air raid shelter, she had the same first name as me and my surname was next to hers on the class register. One of the female teachers always got muddled as to which one of us was which; so when she saw me waiting at the bus stop outside the school the day after the tragedy she stopped to speak to me. She really was very shaken and said that she thought it was me who had died. That one incident made me think more about life and death than any of the bombs and guns had done previously. It really did have a deep effect on me. Over the years I have often thought about the other Iris and wondered what difference it made to the world that I was saved. I was about thirteen and I began to wonder from that moment on what my place in life was about, and why was my life important enough to be saved?[9]

The children in Anna Freud's research study also recounted events that affected them profoundly, and most were touched by the war in some way or another. Some had lost relatives such as fathers, uncles, brothers or cousins who were in the fighting forces, while some of them had experienced the grief of losing family members, friends or neighbours closer to home. The ways in which they dealt with these experiences depended on their age and family support networks. Yet again, the research study concluded that if children were able to talk about their loss and their fears to family members then they were able to follow the normal pattern of grief.

Those who were unable to talk things through suppressed their feelings and developed long-term psychological problems. Such manifestations of suppressed grief usually resulted in regressive behaviour and withdrawal. Evacuated children were more often the emotional and psychological casualties in this respect, since many of them did not feel able to discuss their feelings with strangers. Indeed, this stockpiling and suppression of childhood emotions resulted in a proliferation of child guidance clinics in the post-war years. In part, this proliferation occurred because the professional discipline of child psychology had at long last been validated, but also because the numbers of children who had obviously been affected by wartime events were too numerous to ignore. Henceforth, child welfare officers were expected to gauge a child's psychological state in addition to their physical wellbeing.

Moreover, new child guidance clinics quickly reaffirmed Freud's initial research observations; namely that those children who had endured long separations from their parents as a result of evacuation experienced intense psychological problems. City children, who had stayed with their families for the duration of the war, continued to be more mentally robust. Evacuated children suffered from profound feelings of abandonment, many were frightened of any subsequent form of separation and consequently some developed attachment disorders. In addition, a number of them felt physically sick at the mere thought of travelling by train because it brought back memories of their initial separation and many were plagued with overwhelming insecurities. City children generally experienced fewer psychological problems and those that existed tended to be associated with loud noise and confined spaces. For example, a number of children experienced claustrophobia and associated the prospect of being in any confined space with the panic, fear and mayhem of air raids.

Child Psychology

The *Housewife* magazine issued common sense advice to its readers with regard to dealing with children in air-raid shelters, stating:

It is no good pretending to older children that raids are of no importance. Far better to reassure them by admitting the danger, but stressing the very long odds against them being hit. Explain that there are over 42,000,000 people in Great Britain, and even if the Germans were better shots than they are, they could only manage to kill a few out of that number, and the chances of your home being hit are therefore extremely small. Also explain that the slightly shaky, sick feeling which they experience during raids is not really being afraid but is the result of the interference with the normal vibrations in the atmosphere due to the explosion. That will help to take away that feeling of guilt that school boys and school girls are apt to experience when they fear they are not being as brave as they would like to be.[10]

There were also differences in the time span of illnesses and coping strategies of children with psychological disorders. The sense of abandonment experienced by evacuated children tended to be a long-term psychological issue that was far harder to confront and treat than that of the noise and confined space phobias of city children. But as one gentleman who lived through the Blitz recalled:

We didn't know any different. To us it was normal. After one particularly heavy raid I remember looking at my mother and saying 'What's wrong?' because she looked more worried than usual. We had been sheltering under the stairs during the raid. She looked at me and replied very calmly, 'No need to worry, the house has just fallen down around us that's all.' Well, as a seven year old boy you just accept it. Rescuers came and got us out. They had to remove part of the wall brick by brick until there was enough space for us to crawl out of the rubble. We simply accepted things and people helped each other.[11]

Some indication of the normality of children's behaviour can be gleaned from the diaries of Eileen Potter, a social worker who was given the task of transporting children in various cohorts and by various means out of London once the Blitz had begun:

Sunday 5 November

Rise at about 6.15 am as I have to be at a school in Hammersmith at 7.30 to assemble a party of children to be evacuated to Somerset. It is just getting light as I arrive. We stow ourselves on the coach as best we can and finally set out at about 9 o'clock. There are twenty-four children, a voluntary escort and myself, and also the driver's grown up daughter, who is travelling with us as far as Wiltshire. I make room for myself amongst the luggage on the back seat. We have about a hundred and forty miles journey ahead of us. Most of the children are rather big but there is a sprinkling of smaller ones, including an unaccompanied three year old, who turns out to be the success of the party, chatting and laughing all the way, except when asleep.

One boy embarks upon a vivid description of the film The Spy in Black, but becomes involved in an argument with another boy regarding some of the details of the plot. Another boy keeps asking questions about rabbits, pheasants, etc. in the various parts of the country. It transpires that he has been given an air gun as a present and wants to know what he may shoot with it. Going along the Great West Road, we are stopped for a few minutes by a 'speed cop', as we have been slightly exceeding thirty miles an hour.

When we get about as far as Slough, the first complaints of sickness are heard. There is a family party, two brothers and a sister sitting near the front of the coach together. One of the boys sets the ball rolling, and he and his sister keep on being sick in turn at intervals throughout the journey. The younger sister of one of the technical school girls boasts that she is never sick, but that her elder sister always feels sick when travelling by coach. The big girl says that she thinks she will be alright, but ultimately succumbs, and is sick two or three times. Fairly frequent stops have to be made to empty the receptacles provided.

At last we reach our destination, a small watering place on the Bristol Channel. By now it has begun to rain, and a chilly wind is blowing. The place looks rather desolate, and I feel I could not blame the children if they wanted to go straight home again.[12]

Arguments, playfulness, competitiveness and sickness all conspired to make a journey tedious, but at least some groups of children were reasonably compliant when collected, others were literally dragged away kicking and screaming:

Friday 15 December

Go to see some children off by ambulance from one of the Hammersmith schools. We go first to North Kensington to pick up two small boys. The elder one at first says he will not come, and begins to cry, but is pacified when his mother gives him a toy policeman filled with sweets.

We go on to another house near Shepherds Bush – a much cleaner and prosperous type of home – to pick up two more children, a boy and a girl. They both declare that they will not leave mummy and daddy, and kick and struggle and scream when put in the car. All three children are put into the back seat and locked safely in, whilst Miss X and I sit in the front. We drive off, the children still screaming in the rear, and several of the neighbours looking on. Gradually the sounds of sobbing subside, and I look round to find them beginning to sit up and look around them. When we come to Clapham Common, they murmur, 'We're in the country in a car!' Presently they begin to sing 'Run Adolf Run, and something is said about rabbits, from which I conclude that they think Adolf is some kind of rabbit.[13]

Certainly, many children did manage to settle down with host families once they were taken into reception areas, especially during the second wave of evacuation. A percentage of these children even found better homes than they had hitherto experienced, but from a psychological standpoint they also suffered invisible emotional scars to a far greater degree than those who were left in the cities with their families.

One 3-and-a-half-year-old boy in Freud's nursery compulsively put his coat on and off as if to go out, and sat mourning for his absent mother, refusing to play with other children until she was able to visit him. A 4-year-old girl sat for several days on the exact spot where her mother had left her, would not eat, speak or play and had to be moved around like an automaton.[14]

Through her painstaking research and innovative approaches to child psychology, Anna Freud did establish that the strength and endurance of emotional ties between children and their parents far outweighed other factors in terms of influencing overall child development. Moreover, she argued that the importance of this child–parent bond could not be overstated. The presence or absence of this bond was therefore crucial to child health, and it explained why children continued to thrive well in cities despite the appalling conditions caused by the Blitz. Naturally, responses to war and its associated trauma, loss and grief varied widely amongst all children. But contrary to popular belief at the time, Freud's groundbreaking research proved without any doubt that children living in the cities throughout the war coped far better mentally, emotionally and physically than their evacuee counterparts. In doing so, her research also proved that emotional, psychological and physical developments in children were inextricably linked. Thus, city children who were surrounded by their family members were bound to develop quicker than their homesick evacuee counterparts in the country. The latter group may have had fresher air, more sleep and better food, but they were also emotionally bereft. The mystifying child development reports with regard to height and weight that had confounded government ministers were, thanks to Freud, no longer a mystery. They had simply provided the first evidence that alongside nutritional and environmental concerns, emotional ties were an essential component in child development. As another psychologist from the Freud school of thought, Edward Glover, observed, 'Long drawn out states of homesickness, upset and despair were observed (as a result of wartime separation), compared with which the mental conditions of children sleeping on the Underground was a state of bliss to which all children desired to return.'[15]

Notes

1   Hansard House of Commons Parliamentary Debates, 5th Series, 30 June 1942, report of the Supply Committee.
2   Garfield, S., *We Are at War* (2005), p. 204.
3   Ibid., p. 224.
4   Ibid., p. 340.
5   Ibid., p. 349.
6   Freud, A., *War and Children* (1943), p. 178.

7   National Archive ED/50/206, memo to the Board of Education: 'Nervous Strain in Children', 1941.

8   Parsons, M. and Starns, P, *Evacuation: The True Story* (1999), p. 95.

9   Oral history testimony: Williams, Iris, 17 May 2011.

10 Gardiner, J., *The Blitz: The British Under Attack* (2010), p. 194.

11 G.W., *City on Fire*, HTV production, 2000.

12 Garfield, S., *We Are at War* (2005), p. 76

13 Ibid., p. 122.

14 Gardiner, J., *The Blitz: The British Under Attack* (2010), p. 194.

15 Ibid., p. 198–9.

The Bristol Blitz

*I*n 1939, as Britain prepared for war, Bristol parents were not given the choice as to whether or not to evacuate their children to the countryside. Given its geographical position the Anderson Committee had afforded the city neutral status. Such status dictated that Bristol was not required to receive any evacuees, but neither were they required to move their children to places of greater safety. Anderson had reasoned that Nazi war planes would not be able to reach the city from their bases in Germany, and wrongly believed that France would hold out against a German invasion. Once France succumbed to the Nazis however, German planes were able to use French air bases to launch air strikes, particularly in Paris. Consequently, Bristol was subjected to fierce and sustained bombing. The main targets were the docks of Bristol and Avonmouth, the railway station at Temple Meads and the region's aerodrome at Filton. As the location of the Bristol Aeroplane Company (now British Aerospace) the latter was responsible for the production of Bristol Blenheim and Beaufighter aircraft, and the Luftwaffe intended to destroy the aerodrome factory, runways and aircraft. Although throughout the war only eight aircraft were destroyed beyond repair, and on one occasion the Luftwaffe bombed a factory in South Wales instead of Filton by mistake!

Bristol's Blitz began on 25 June 1940 and bombing continued with varying intensity until 15 May 1944. The initial lack of civilian evacuation procedures prompted Bristolians to initiate their own unique civil defence procedures in response to air-raid bombardments, and the subsequent destruction of their homes. Fortunately, Bristol was blessed with an abundance of very old churches that could hold hundreds of people in their crypts. As soon as the warning sirens sounded across the city and the anti-aircraft fire began to fill the air with what people termed as the 'ack ack' sound, large sections of the population headed for their local churches. But while the ancient crypts saved many, such as the 300 who escaped an incendiary fire at St Michael's church, others were not so lucky, and when the church of St Barnabas was hit the bomb fell directly on the crypt, killing fifteen people. People also took shelter in disused railway tunnels, castle dungeons and shop cellars. Some decided to walk out to the surrounding hills each night and watch the dog fights from the relative safety of the Mendips. Hostels were established to offer shelter to those whose homes were destroyed by the bombs and many of these included large communal air-raid shelters.

A Bristol gentleman who was a small boy when the Blitz began remembered the time as traumatic, but simultaneously exciting and interesting:

I was six years old when the war started. I was born in the Bedminster area of Bristol. My father worked on the buses and then went into the army when the war began – he was in the military police. I used to stay with my grandmother in Stokes Croft at week-ends, my grandparents owned a shoe shop in the area and they used to live above it. When the bombs first started dropping it must have been a week-end because I was with my grandmother and my mother was in a pub off Castle Street playing darts. My grandmother ushered me down to her coal shelter and we were okay that night. I wasn't frightened because I was with my grandmother and she seemed to be calm. Sometime later I used to watch the dog fights from my grandmother's shop. The whole of Bristol was bombed and one night when the bombing got very close my grandmother decided that we needed to get out of the shop. The local hostel was full and the shelters were full up. Brunswick Square was on fire and we were also near a main gas works. My grandmother's dog was a Great Dane and one night when an incendiary bomb landed in the press room of the shoe shop and started a fire, the dog actually put it out with one of its paws – I'll never forget that. Anyway, that particular night we walked all the way from Stokes Croft in Bristol to my grandmother's sisters' country house in Hanham, it was about ten miles I think. We stayed there for a couple of days and then came back to the shoe shop.

There was rubble everywhere and police had roped off some places where there were unexploded bombs, and areas where building structures were unsafe. Bombs must have hit some sewers because there were rats climbing up pipes and running along walls. Some of the houses were very old you see – and there used to be two parks around there – any rate some young lads used to shoot at them with air pistols and catapults. There was also a fat Italian man who used to pay young boys to catch pigeons for him. He owned a pet shop, but I don't know why he wanted the pigeons, I only know that he used to sell them on to folk.

I stayed in Bristol for the duration of the war and my whole family survived. We always slept with our clothes on because you never knew when the bombs might come, and often it would be in the middle of the night. I was lucky because I was never ill, even though we ate a lot of bread and dripping and dried egg. I didn't go to school much because there were no air raid shelters at my school and then everything was bombed so there was not much left. I had holes in my shoes even though my grandparents had a shoe shop and made shoes. There was a shortage of raw materials until the Yanks came, so we put cardboard in our shoes to cover the holes. Once the Yanks came things were better. We children used to follow them around because they gave us chewing gum. The young women liked them too because they gave them stockings. Rubber came into the shoe shop very quickly once the Yanks arrived, it all had U.S.A. stamped on it and my granddad was very busy making the boots and shoes for the American Army. There was also a company nearby that made rubber raincoats. In fact I went to work for Anderson's rubber company after the war.

I do not remember being frightened during the blitz, I was always with my mother or grandmother and they didn't seem to be frightened. They just took it in their stride – except for the night we walked to Hanham. I think my grandmother was a bit scared that night, the Germans; they were heading for the aerodrome you see. But as children the war was just part of our childhood, we didn't know any different. I remember we had sweet coupons, and the sweet shop near us displayed all the sweets openly, so as to entice the children I suppose; and I will never forget the sight – although it was quite normal – of little mice running around amongst the sweets in the shop window. It was quite funny to watch.

We used to play rounders in the streets with an old tennis racket, boys against the girls, and a game called five stones. Any old stones would do. We'd put four on the floor and throw one up in the air and see how many of the others we could pick up. We also had yo-yos, marbles, and we played conkers. The cinemas stayed open and all we children went there on Saturday mornings. I remember we watched Tarzan films a lot. We also used to go train-spotting with our little pencils and bits of paper. Some of the boys would say that they had seen the King George train but most of them hadn't, because it didn't go by very often. A few of the boys would boast about the number of trains they'd seen and that sort of thing, we were just like any normal children.[1]

Whilst this gentleman remembered feeling reassured by the presence of his family during the bombing raids, this was not the case for all children. David Gay recalled that he always sheltered with his parents but this did not take away his fear:

I felt frightened to death when the bombs came over; it was like all hell being let loose. The bombs caused a gas explosion somewhere, and bombs were dropped on a paraffin warehouse. I went to Staple Hill school and one night everything else was bombed in the area, but not the school. After a bombing raid my Dad would point out the places where I was not allowed to play – he'd point his finger and say 'Now don't you go mucking about over there.' My father never seemed to be worried about any of it. Every night he just used to stand there and watch the aeroplanes. Sometimes we would go out of Bristol onto a hill and look down on the city I felt that it was ok to watch the aeroplanes then because I felt safer.[2]

By the end of November 1940 even the most stoical of Bristolians were beginning to wilt under the pressure of persistent aerial bombardment. Temple Meads railway station had been bombed, along with Bristol Cathedral School, the famous Wills cigarette factory, the ancient heartland of the city with its beautiful seventeenth-century buildings, the docks and surrounding settlements, St Peters Hospital and church, and the much-loved historic Temple church. In addition, acres of homes were destroyed and prime shopping sites were completely wiped out. Official casualty rates rose dramatically and firefighting equipment was commandeered from Cardiff, Plymouth and other surrounding areas as Bristol prepared for further onslaughts.

Rhoda Edmonds was a teacher in the city when the bombs began raining down and recalled the frantic efforts to protect the city's children alongside the bravery and resilience of ordinary Bristolians:

I was twenty one when war broke out and although I was trained to teach fourteen year olds my first job was teaching primary school girls in Knowle West. But I was only there for a short time when I was transferred to a large school for senior children near Lawrence Hill railway station. The Headmaster was very strict. There were masters and boys on the first floor and mistresses and girls on the ground floor, and we were not allowed to mix, he was very particular about that rule. During the Dunkirk retreat a trainload of soldiers were brought to Stapleton Road station and because of the lack of accommodation on the first night they returned, a lot of soldiers were left to sleep in Eastville Park. The senior girls went back and forth from their homes to give them food and drinks. Some of the girls even gave up their beds and slept on the floor so that the soldiers could have a good nights sleep. They eventually found accommodation for the soldiers at Frenchay.

Anyway, now that France had gone the air raids became frequent. We were told to listen for a whistle that would alert us to the planes coming over – but we had a big problem because the school was near the railway station, and with the old steam trains the guard would blow the whistle every time the train was about to set off so my senior girls were a bag of nerves! One day the Headmaster said that the German planes were very near and told us 'It sounds very much like they are after Filton airfield.' We rushed to the church crypt up the road and it was a bad raid. One shelter was completely destroyed. We always sheltered in the church crypt. Sometimes we were able to sit on upright tombs but other times we were so packed that we all had to stand.

In November 1940 there was a very severe attack and the centre of Bristol was completely ruined. My teenage girls were old enough to realise what was happening but the little children were very scared and didn't always understand what was happening. An incendiary bomb crashed through the roof of my bedroom on one occasion and landed just inches from my bed. Luckily I was not in at the time. But everyone was very helpful nearly all of the time. They did whatever they could for each other and were very considerate of other people's needs. If there was anything they could do then they would do it. Most of the Bristol people took turns to firewatch even when they were very tired and had jobs to do next morning. Having something to do – something to keep you occupied stopped you from being frightened. There were two men, who owned a green grocer's shop near me, and one man was in his little garden by his shop one day and he didn't get into our communal shelter in time and he received a direct hit. I knew him very well and that was the nearest in terms of personal tragedy that the war got to me.[3]

At the height of the November bombing there were over seventy major fires burning in the centre of Bristol at any given time, but as Bristolians bought their daily newspaper looking for details of the air strikes wartime censorship rules precluded any real information. For instance, severe and prolonged raids took place on Sunday 24 November and most of the medieval part of the city centre was destroyed on this fearful night. The severity of the situation could be gauged by the fact that a vicar conducting his service in St Peter's Church near the centre solemnly announced to his congregation that they would probably all die that night. He then proceeded to continue with the service as the Luftwaffe flew over the city destroying all in their path. Yet the following day the headlines in the *Bristol Evening Post* simply announced that a 'West Town has been Bombed'. A married couple who were in the city on that night remembered their lucky escape:

We were courting at the time and when the planes came over we thought we had time to get home. But we started running and my wife kept telling me that her stockings were falling down, I said never mind your stockings, the bombs are falling down! An ARP warden came across to us and said you'd better come into the shelter because this looks like its going to be a heavy raid. I told him that we wanted to carry on walking to get back to my Dad because he was at home alone, but he persuaded us to come into the shelter anyway. A few seconds later a bomb dropped just at the place where we would have been walking if we had carried on and ignored the advice of the ARP warden. We stayed in the shelter all night and when we came out in the morning ours was the only shelter in the road that was still standing. We were very lucky that night. Hundreds were killed and it would have been much worse if it had been any other night. The fact that it was a Sunday meant that a lot of people had stayed at home.[4]

On 16 December the king arrived in Bristol on a morale-boosting mission. He toured the city with the mayor and was sympathetic to the plight of Bristolians. The centre of the city was in ruins by this stage and its hardy citizens were desperate for some respite. Air raids had left mounds of rubble, unstable buildings, burst water mains, torn telephone wires and electric cables, and frayed nerves. Furthermore, amid the ensuing chaos, as everyone prepared for the Christmas festivities the bombing continued unabated. Rhoda Edmonds described how events and instructions for everyone, including teachers, could change at a moments notice:

I went home to Monmouthshire for Christmas 1940 and was preparing to return to Bristol on the fifth day of my holiday when a telegram arrived. It stated simply STAY HOME WAR DAMAGE. Well, I took off my hat and coat and thought I might as well have a cup of tea and relax a bit. No sooner had I done that when another knock came at the door with a second telegram, this one said STAFF NEEDED FOR SALVAGE WORK so I put my hat and coat back on and set off again. I had missed the train I was originally going to catch and so I cycled to the next junction. I handed my bike to a porter with instructions for him to give the bike to my sister Agnes who was a land girl in the area. At any rate somebody must have telephoned to say that I was on my way because they held up the Bristol train for me, and I managed to get the train as far as Lawrence Hill. The school should have been there but it wasn't. It had been a frosty moonlit night when the planes had come over and the school was flattened. A big fire had burnt all the desks. Try to imagine us all walking in the morning after the raid when everything was frozen. The children had nowhere to go. We had a lot of meetings and eventually a nearby school doubled up and gave us two rooms for the girls and two for the boys. There was a shortage of everything and a big problem with children's clothes and shoes. In one family a brother and sister used to take turns to wear one pair of shoes, and one would come to school wearing them in the morning and the other in the afternoon. But the worst thing was when the water, electricity and gas pipes were bombed because we had nothing to cook with and had to carry around buckets of water and take it in turns to be the first to wash in one bowl of water!

Most of the children coped very well and they stayed surprisingly healthy. I did feel very sorry for them though. They didn't know what it was like to taste bananas and they couldn't have many sweets. By 1941 some of the cinemas were bombed so they had little in the way of entertainment. The parks were full of big shelters and the metal railings and other equipment had been taken down to be used for the war effort. I must admit that I had been getting on quite well with my ice skating at Bristol ice rink before the war but they closed it down and then all of that area was badly bombed. Things got so bad in Bristol that a lot of people were saying that we needed to get the little children especially, out of the city. The problem was that we had nowhere really to send them. We weren't an evacuation area you see, and most of the accommodation was already taken up by others. Devon said that they would take some children, but only if they could reserve the right to send Bristol teachers wherever they liked.[5]

In January 1941 the city's Lord Mayor Alderman T.H.J. Underdown initiated consultations with the Minister of Health, Mr Malcolm Macdonald, with a view to organising some evacuation plan for Bristol children. Mr MacDonald duly visited the city in the same month to survey the seriousness of the situation. Bristol's mayor was also tireless in his efforts to press the government to change Bristol's status from a neutral to an evacuation area, since this would immediately generate more government assistance in terms of civilian protection. But Bristol's status was never changed and in effect the city's officials were pretty much left to their own devices.

One such official, named C.M. MacInnes, was given forty-eight hours to compile a report detailing the opinions and general morale of the city's population with regard to the bombing and the prospect of evacuation. With unremitting air raids taking their toll on people's livelihoods and lifestyles there were considerable fears that low morale could potentially lead to subversive activity. In compiling his report MacInnes relied heavily on members of the clergy and social workers, Rotary Club members and other voluntary organisations for specific information. After a brief deliberation due to time constraints he concluded that some measures, designed to assist civilians during the bombing, were failing to help those who were most in need. There was also a significant social class divide in certain areas. MacInnes discovered that roughly 30 per cent of the population took to the hills every night but this exodus was often dependent on the availability of transport and the finances of individuals. Generally people were helpful to their neighbours, but apparently there were a few lorry drivers who were less public-spirited and insisted on charging as much as 1s for each person attempting to flee the city. Those who were living in poorer areas and those with small children simply could not afford these fares. Consequently they either remained in Bristol to face the wrath of the bombers or trekked miles into the countryside on foot. MacInnes reported in very sombre tones that this disorganised ad hoc evacuation was likely to cause a great deal of class bitterness and could prepare the ground for defeatism and subversive propaganda. There were concerns that a few people were also obtaining petrol on the black market, which enabled them to travel out of the city each night. Not surprisingly the unfairness of this situation rankled communities and caused divisions. Some firewatchers also expressed grievances because many of them had volunteered to guard homes and factories but were disappointed that the factory owners did not often watch alongside them – preferring instead to take refuge in the surrounding villages while their employees kept watch. But he reported that, as with other services, more men were happy to volunteer for firewatching and guarding homes during the raids if they could be assured that their own wives and children were safe.[6]

MacInnes' hastily compiled report was highly influential and underlined the need for a more co-ordinated official response to the bombing. As one charity official complained:

> In the course of our work we are, since the heavy raids, constantly receiving requests to help families to move out of these particularly dangerous areas. In every case the request has been quite reasonable, either there is chronic illness in the family or large numbers of small children or the husband is on active service so that it is difficult or dangerous for them to avail themselves of the protection of the Anderson shelter.[7]

By 16 March the air raids had claimed the lives of over 600 people and injured nearly 2,000 – over half of these were seriously injured. Then, on the night of the 16th, Bristol suffered the worst raid of the war: 250 people were killed and nearly 400 injured between 8.30 p.m. and 4.15 a.m. According to the *Western Daily Press* approximately 800 high-explosive bombs had been dropped on the city during that period, along with thousands of incendiary bombs.

Yet more unremitting bombardments followed these intense and highly destructive air raids. The heavy April raids, which elderly Bristolians still refer to as the 'Good Friday raids', claimed nearly 200 lives and inflicted 400 injuries. The targets once more were the docks and the aerodrome. In his role of chancellor of the University of Bristol, the prime minister visited Bristol on 12 April 1941 and praised the city's civil defence workers:

> Many of those here today have been all night at their posts and have all been under the fire of the enemy, under heavy and protracted bombardment. That you should gather in this way is a mark of fortitude and phlegm, of a courage and detachment from worldly affairs. I go about the country whenever I can escape for a few hours or a day from my headquarters, and I see the damage done by enemy attacks: but I also see side by side with the devastation and amid the ruins a consciousness of being associated with a cause far higher and wider than any human or personal issue. I see the spirit of an unconquerable people.[8]

There was no doubt that Bristol City Council officials, along with members of the clergy voluntary organisations such as the British Red Cross and social workers, did their utmost to improve the lot of Bristolians. But all available shelters were eventually overflowing with panic-stricken people. Some 3,000 Bristolians had taken refuge in a disused railway tunnel that ran under Brunel's famous suspension bridge. Organised bedding arrangements in the shape of a three-tier bunk system and basic refreshments deliveries had, by now, taken the place of chaotic ad hoc measures. Moreover, when BBC officials tried to evict people from the tunnel in order to use the space for broadcasting, these same people wrote to the queen to protest – this move prompted the BBC to abandon all eviction efforts. Bristolians had trusted the queen to respond to their plight and they were duly rewarded. They remained defiant against the enemy bombers and their belief in their monarchy, country and an eventual victory sustained their morale. By acting on MacInnes' recommendations for a more co-ordinated civil defence strategy the mayor was also able to implement hasty evacuation schemes. Appealing to rural councils he arranged for some of the younger children to go to Dorset and further south to Devon, but most children remained behind in the city. In part this was due to a shortage of accommodation in the countryside, yet evidence also suggests that the majority of parents had decided to see the war out together with their children.

Iris Williams remembered that at this point in the war both she and her sister were offered the chance to go and live in the country to escape the air raids:

> My mother asked both of us if we wanted to leave Bristol because of all the bombing. I didn't want to go. I didn't like change and the war had already brought about too many changes for my liking, what with my school being bombed. I could tell that my mother didn't want us to go anywhere and I didn't want to upset her. My sister said that she had thought for a fleeting moment that perhaps leaving Bristol might have been an adventure but then she thought better of it and she decided that she wanted to stay too.[9]

Certainly by the time Bristol evacuation procedures were firmly in place in the summer of 1941 the worst of the bombing was over. Once the British Royal Air Force had defeated the German Luftwaffe during the Battle of Britain, Hitler abandoned his invasion plans for Britain and turned his attention eastwards. Rhoda Edmonds eventually ended up in a little village near Portishead on the outskirts of Bristol with a band of children that she had not known before her excursion out of the city. 'We could watch the planes come over from there and it was a safe distance. We were across the river but some of the Bristol people still used to come out of the city each night to find safety in the surrounding villages.'[10]

Like most other major British cities most of the German bombs that fell during the Bristol Blitz came between June 1940 and June 1941. Random bombing raids occurred until the end of May 1944. However, in terms of shock and tragedy most Bristolians recall a single incident, which occurred in August 1942, when without warning one morning a German bomber dropped a hefty bomb on the Broad Weir area of the city. This bomb tragically landed on three buses that were carrying mainly women and their children, killing forty-five passengers and severely injuring fifty-six. Brave firefighters who rushed to the tragic scene were at a complete loss because there was very little they could do. This appalling tragedy left an indelible mark on the public consciousness at the time, and is still remembered vividly by elderly members of Bristol's population; primarily because there was no warning siren on that occasion, and the main victims were the city's innocent children.

From that time on the bombing continued in fits and starts until May 1944, when the last of Hitler's bombs fell on the beleaguered city of Bristol. Only then could the city's population turn their attention towards the arduous work of reconstruction. As a tribute to the everyday wartime bravery and heroic resilience of Bristolians, a number of beautiful stained glass windows were erected in the majestic Bristol cathedral. They commemorate the courageous efforts of the firefighters, voluntary services and civil defence workers who fought to save their historic city from destruction, and protect its citizens from the fury of the enemy.

Above and following illustrations: Stained-glass windows in the north aisle of Bristol Cathedral, depicting the Women's Voluntary Services, the Wardens' Service, the Home Guard and the British Red Cross Society. (By kind permission of the Dean and Chapter of Bristol Cathedral)

Notes

1 Oral history testimony: anonymous, 13 April 2011.
2 Ibid.: Gay, David, 13 April 2011.
3 Ibid.: Edmonds, Rhoda, 20 April 2011.
4 *City on Fire*, HTV production, 2000.
5 Oral history testimony: Edmonds, Rhoda, 20 April 2011.
6 Report of C.M. MacInnes to Bristol City Council, January 1941, extracts taken from Parsons, M. and Starns, P., *Evacuation: The True Story* (1999), p. 50–2.
7 Ibid.
8 Prime Minister Winston Churchill speaking at the University of Bristol, 12 April 1941, quoted in Gardiner, J., *The Blitz: The British Under Attack* (2010) p. 267.
9 Oral history testimony: Williams, Iris, 21 May 2011.
10 Ibid.: Edmonds, Rhoda, 20 April 2011.

The Plymouth Blitz

Like the city of Bristol, Plymouth began the war as a designated neutral area. Unlike Bristol however, Plymouth managed to get its status changed to that of an evacuation area at the height of the Blitz. Thus, albeit rather late in the day, the Ministry of Health stepped in to help the citizens of Plymouth with their civilian evacuation procedures. Moreover, official records reveal that there were two primary reasons why Plymouth succeeded in changing its status and why Bristol failed in this respect.

Firstly, the question of maintaining morale seemed to be afforded a higher priority in Plymouth. As home of the Royal Marine Barracks the Royal Naval Barracks and the Royal Dockyard, Plymouth was a vital military base. However, the Home Intelligence Service, which monitored levels of morale in a clandestine fashion throughout the war, voiced concerns about the population of Plymouth during the Blitz. Apparently, although morale generally was considered to be extraordinarily good, there was also a lot of defeatist talk in some quarters. This was a particularly worrying trend in an area that contained a large number of naval families.[1] Commanders in the British armed forces had previously warned government ministers in no uncertain terms that in order for men to fight well in the theatre of battle, it was important for these same men to know that their families were safe. As a crucial naval establishment, therefore, it was imperative to the overall war effort that morale in Plymouth remained high and unwavering. There was no room for defeatist talk of any kind.

Secondly, Plymouth was very fortunate in having an extremely vocal and well-connected Conservative MP in the shape of Viscountess Nancy Astor. This honourable lady had also become the city's mayoress in 1939 when her husband Lord Astor assumed the role of mayor. As an MP Lady Astor was an outspoken, witty, intelligent and vibrant woman, who was a staunch advocate for child welfare – both in her own constituency of Plymouth Sutton and in the country as a whole. Renowned for her almost love–hate relationship with Prime Minister Winston Churchill, she was outspoken in the House of Commons and forceful in her approach to politics, particularly in the field of women's rights and child health. But she was viewed with suspicion by some in Whitehall; in part because of her unflinching support for the pre-war appeasement of Germany, in part because she was American by birth. Despite the fact that Lady Astor subsequently voted against Chamberlain in order to bring Churchill to power, and admitted with considerable frankness that she had been mistaken in her support of appeasement, there were those who could not quite forgive her error in this respect.

Furthermore, at times she seemed to court disaster by making glaringly unjust and sweeping statements in some of her parliamentary speeches and by adopting less than conventional religious affiliations. However, as the first lady to ever take up a seat in Parliament, and in terms of representing her constituents, Lady Astor was undoubtedly committed to Plymouth. Indeed, she argued vociferously and continuously on their behalf throughout the war and was instrumental in getting the official status of Plymouth changed from neutral to evacuation area once the Blitz began. This process of changing Plymouth's status was, nonetheless, a slow one.

In the meantime the population took to sheltering in the surrounding countryside at night, in much the same way as their counterparts were doing in Bristol whenever a raid occurred. But sometimes there was no warning. On 17 March 1941, for instance, eight bombs dropped on a playing field in Devonport, killing a number of the boys who had been leisurely playing football only moments earlier.[2] A few days later, on the 20th, the city's hospital was among the many buildings that were bombed in a relentless raid that lasted almost four hours. Four nurses and nineteen children were killed. The latter were listed as follows in the Imperial War Graves Commission records:

Michael John Birdman aged twenty one months; Derek Blatchford aged two years; John Blatchford, aged three years, Angela Earle, aged four months; Philip Eve, aged two years; Terence Michael Fox, aged twenty three months; Peter Hamlyn, aged four months; Leslie Frank Hogg, aged ten days; Alan John Jones-Burnell, aged two years; twins Maureen and Nicholas John Lowndes-Millward, aged ten months; Albert Michael McManus, aged twenty one months; Charles Matthews, aged eighteen months; Susan Peacock, aged three months; Pauline May Sharland, aged one month; Winifred Valerie Shears, aged twenty three months; Shirley Short, aged two years; Phyllis Taylor, aged eleven months, and Harold Santilla, who, at a mere seven days old was the youngest of the victims.[3]

To lose so many very young children in one night was an extreme tragedy for the citizens of Plymouth, most of whom were suffering from severe shock. The king and queen, who had recently visited the city, sent a message to Lady Astor expressing their deep sympathy and the local authority issued emergency measures to evacuate as many children as possible. Virtually all of Plymouth had been bombed and by the early hours of 21 March the whole city was on fire. The bombing continued the following night and enemy planes managed to destroy St Andrews Church and all of the municipal buildings, including the Guildhall. Schools were flattened and one teacher recalled that the evacuation measures were so impromptu that nobody was entirely sure of the procedures:

I was told to take a coach load of children to Coverack but the only way of contacting the children was to scour the individual shelters and beg their mothers to part with them. The countryside was already so full of children from other cities but the authority had managed to get hold of a large country house and we were told to try and take the youngest ones with us. The morning before we were supposed to leave I remember spending a very dark and difficult night trying to track down the children. It was pitiful really, to see all the pathetic little bundles clinging to their mothers for dear life. I wanted to take all of them but there was only room for about thirty on my coach, and some mothers wanted to keep their children with them, especially if they were toddlers or babies.[4]

Another teacher had a similar experience:

During that time the blitz was extremely bad, particularly where my children lived. On the Sunday night my friend and I went amongst all the blitzed houses where the children had been night after night, telling them all to meet us at the railway station the next day. We got on the train on the Monday and landed in Cambourne. We were all turfed out and the children were taken to the school to be examined for dirty heads and impetigo. Farmers came and picked the big boys and girls to work on the farms, but we were not billeted until night time. We eventually ended up in a village called Coverack but we were not always safe. One day my friend Winnie was walking down to the beach with her party of schoolchildren and suddenly a plane appeared over the top of the houses. She said she could see him as plainly as anything, and he dropped four bombs on the village. Several people were killed. The telephone wires and everything came down over our children. But they had been used to ducking for many moons. The plane then proceeded to machine gun people on the beach. Our children were alright but it was a worrying time.[5]

According to Mass Observation reports the civil defence services and evacuation procedures in Plymouth were disorganised and ill-conceived. The population relied too heavily on the navy to come to their rescue rather than organising their own teams in a co-ordinated fashion:

While they recognised that these were exceptionally difficult circumstances, and singled out some individuals, like Public Assistance Officers and those running mobile canteens, for praise, they were generally deeply unimpressed by what they observed of the organisation in the city, and particularly the post raid evacuation, which they described as 'disastrous chaos', 'disgusting, degrading and tantamount to sabotaging the war effort. Who can let things get in such a mess and get away with it?'[6]

There was evidence that mothers were also worrying about whether or not the reception areas were any safer than the cities, and displays of despondency with regard to the war were not uncommon, as expectant mother Tilly Rice recorded in her diary:

Yesterday afternoon I went down to the beach to join the children. It is of course nearly deserted at this time of year, though there were about a dozen people down there, also self evacuees, including a party of three doctor's children sent from Plymouth. Mention was made of the new R.A.F. aerodrome a few miles away, and I wondered if this place was as war-safe as any other, though in my own case it is not the immunity from air raids that is the attraction so much as immunity from war 'atmosphere'. Yesterday evening was spent, as usual on Saturday, listening to Bandwagon. The news was listened to intently but gave rise to little comment. Possibly there would be more discussion here with some provocative remarks thrown out, but I refrain more than I should do ordinarily because when a houseful of strange people are thrown together for an indefinite period, relations should be kept as uncontroversial as possible. I think there is some tendency to anti-German feeling, which I seemed to notice when I mentioned making a German dish this morning. It was rather inclined to be dismissed as 'too rich', and the comment was 'they won't be able to make it nowadays anyway', but otherwise there is very little said excepting for murmurs of 'too dreadful' and 'too marvellous' as various exploits of the enemy and our own men are described on the wireless. My own reactions to the whole situation are growing more and more indifferent every day. I have felt all along that somehow I must get my children out of the way, but were I not expecting another child I would not care where I was. Children will take the place of all those who have been and will be destroyed in the current struggle, though when I observe the same old prejudices and inhibitions cropping up in the generation that has arisen since the last war I wonder how much hope there is for anything in the future.[7]

The Blitz of major cities by the Luftwaffe had engendered some sympathy in reception areas, since hosts were more likely to give children a warmer welcome once the bombing had started than they had done during the phoney war period. However, there were still a minority of hosts who viewed them as unwelcome lodgers. Plymouth children who suffered from emotional disturbances and bed wetting, for instance, were housed in a special hostel, which was nicknamed locally as the 'Hostile'. The chaotic mixing of children from different social backgrounds and lifestyles did result in some culture clashes, but these were often quickly resolved. City children may not have known how to identify plants and animals, light oil lamps, collect water from a pump or operate farm machinery, but they were children just the same. Those who were not suffering from homesickness or dubious billets were just as curious, mischievous and eager to explore their surroundings as the next child.

Fortunately, Plymouth council were able to requisition a large country house to accommodate some of their children, by taking advantage of an organisation named the Anglo-American Relief Fund. This organisation was established thanks to the generosity of the American people. Members sent money and clothes to help bombed-out families, and they provided city children with toys at Christmas and in circumstances where children were literally left with nothing. Dolls were distributed to little girls and toy cars or brightly coloured bricks to young boys. In addition, the British War Relief Society of America also gave a number of valuable grants to city authorities, specifically to help children of the Blitz. Speaking of the plight of Plymouth's children, Lady Astor berated the Ministry of Health for the clumsiness of evacuation arrangements and the belatedness of action:

> The Ministry were supposed to have solid plans, but when it came to the point they had no plans for children. They handed over the evacuation of children to voluntary people. When the children had to be evacuated from Plymouth, the job was handed over to a very nice group who wanted to help their country. A lady came down, with qualifications from the Ministry of Health, to get the children out. Naturally, she did her best, but she knew very little about it, and it was months before anything was done, and even then it was not done on the correct lines. I hope and pray that hon. Members will insist on better care of our children under five years, and see that the problem is faced intelligently. It is a very difficult problem, but our children are precious to us. Every time this country has a defeat in the field, people want an inquiry. I think there ought to be a real inquiry into the policy of the Ministry of Health – whether it is right, whether it is doing what we want to do, whether it is wasting money, whether it is wasting young lives, and whether it could not be improved.[8]

In fairness to the Ministry of Health however, the mass departure of children from evacuation areas had always been viewed as a priority. Plymouth was subjected to delayed evacuation plans simply because the city had been afforded a neutral rather than evacuation status by the Anderson Committee. By the time this status was altered nearly all available billets in the country had been taken by children from other beleaguered cities. Subsequently, as Lady Astor was oft to point out, what everyone in Plymouth needed was a relative in the country. But the lack of rural accommodation dictated that the majority of children still remained in the city long after it was designated an evacuation area.

The population of Plymouth continued, therefore, to make their nightly visits to the countryside and make do as best they could. Some trekked out and set up nightly camps on the bleak terrain of Exmoor and Dartmoor. Approximately 30,000 panic-stricken adults and children escaped the city each night, and in a similar scenario to that of Bristol this situation prompted bad feeling amongst those who were left behind to fight the fires. In an attempt to shore up morale Prime Minister Winston Churchill visited Plymouth in May 1941. By this time the city, like many others, had been flattened. Nevertheless, Plymothians had made concerted efforts to adapt to their circumstances, and civil defence authorities were gradually establishing some sense of order from the rubble and chaos.

The children who remained in Plymouth also quickly adapted to their circumstances. The morning after an air raid, groups of boys could be seen collecting shrapnel from the mud flaps of the river beds. Girls played hopscotch and skipped in the streets as normal and life went on in defiance of the enemy. Cinemas stayed open, as did the dance halls. Church services, fetes, bazaars and youth groups remained a thriving feature of city life. It was also possible to detect a strengthening of parent–child bonds, and as the war progressed children were given a more prominent role within the decision making process of family frameworks. Furthermore, there is evidence that this strengthening of family ties was a growing trend in all children of the Blitz. Whereas before the war parents made the decision with regard to whether or not their children should be evacuated, during the Blitz a surprising number of parents left this decision to their children. As one man, who was 8 at the time, remembered with some affection: 'Instead of being told I had to go to the country, all of a sudden I was being asked whether I wanted to go.'[9]

Since children invariably chose to stay with their parents rather than face the prospect of the unknown, and the fact that most of those who did leave more often than not returned, the numbers of children living in cities actually increased throughout the war. Plymouth was no exception to this trend, and while Lady Astor applauded the people of Plymouth for their spirit and resolve in the face of enemy action, her main sympathy lay with the city's children. Indeed, the level of their suffering during the Blitz prompted her to take the unprecedented step of lobbying Parliament for a Children's Minister; a move that was greeted with laughter and disbelief within the corridors of power. But the detractors did not count on the seriousness of Plymouth's conscientious MP nor on her commitment to child welfare. Speaking in 1942, a frustrated Lady Astor with her patience wearing thin, reiterated her concern about the lack of adequate nurseries for children and the lack of a cohesive policy towards their care:

It is past a joke. If you want to get this thing straight, we ought to have one Parliamentary Secretary whose duty is nothing else but child care. People who come from abroad and inquire about child welfare, say there is no one to whom they can go and ask what is happening to children in the country, because no one knows. The Minister let child minders go by. I was asked to go to Southport to urge women to send their children to child minders. Needless to say, I did not accept. This scheme has failed completely and everybody knows it. When the Parliamentary Secretary went to Plymouth I doubt if she even asked whether anyone in the dockyard wanted nurseries for their children. The Ministry ought to find out in the industrial parts of the country whether there are provisions for the children. But what matters is the future. It will not be possible to change this policy so quickly after the war. I hope that the Minister will believe me when I say that many of us who care desperately about this matter are truly alarmed.[10]

One of the most alarming trends that had resulted from a lack of adequate nurseries in Plymouth and elsewhere was the growing practice of baby sitting. In many instances, family circumstances dictated that mothers needed to go out to work. If they could not find nursery places for their children then they would leave them with a woman who, for a fee, would take care of them while they worked. The level of childcare meted out however, varied enormously. Often, the supposed 'carer' would have large numbers of children and no qualifications in childcare of any description. There were no restrictions on the numbers of children a carer could take in on a daily basis and the lack of regulatory supervision in this respect frequently resulted in child neglect and abuse.

With most of the government ministers naturally preoccupied with the overall war effort and global theatres of battle, it was little wonder that matters of childcare took a back seat in terms of priority. Efforts to determine a coherent policy with regard to nursery provision and the question of directing mothers into war work were often met with conflicting responses. The Ministry of Labour were eager to encourage all women into work, while the Ministry of Health frowned upon mothers returning to work if their children were under the age of 2. Lady Astor frequently locked horns with Parliamentary Secretary for Health Miss Horsbrugh, however, in matters of policy. Since the former was frustrated by the poor quality of childcare in some nurseries and the lack of adequate health provision for city children. But Lady Astor's questions were usually preceded by some praise for existing government efforts and an apology for having to voice criticism. Justifying her campaign to improve childcare, she announced in the House of Commons:

> I, like many other Members of Parliament, do not like criticising the Government just for fun. This is no time to criticise the Government, with the battle in the Middle East going on. We feel that we ought to be a united nation, and we are, I think, united. But I would like to find out from the Government – and this is a question for the House of Commons – what is their policy for the children under five? All of a sudden, a tremendous interest is being shown in juveniles. It has taken a war to do this, as it took the last war to discover what you could really do with young people.[11]

With her incessant parliamentary lobbying on the subject of children there was no doubt that Lady Astor was a self-appointed champion of childcare issues and it was her experience of watching and monitoring the lives of children in blitzed Plymouth that added momentum to her efforts. In addition to her support for better nurseries and qualified nursery workers, Lady Astor also lobbied for family allowances and better education for the under-5s. In a series of fervent parliamentary speeches she outlined an extensive framework for childcare and vehemently declared her contempt for the way in which Germany and Italy had indoctrinated their young: 'The totalitarian governments have always tried to begin with the children. The reason in their case is revolting because they educate them purely for the purpose of fighting.'[12]

British children she argued, especially those who were living through the Blitz, deserved to be educated for a wide variety of purposes in life.[13] But ministers needed to lay the foundation stones for adequate childcare in order for them to have a brighter and more secure future. Therefore, as Plymothians buried their war dead and eventually erected monuments to their military heroes, it was perhaps some consolation for them to know that their children's experience of the Blitz had initiated a wave of unstinting support for child welfare issues. Furthermore, that their own elected MP, Lady Astor had championed child welfare rights, not only for the blitzed children of Plymouth, but for children across the length and breadth of Britain.

Notes

1   *Secrets of the Blitz*, Testimony Film Productions, Steve Humphries, first broadcast 22 January 2011.
2   Ibid.
3   Imperial War Graves Commission: The Civilian War Dead of Plymouth. For more information about this raid please consult Wasley, G., *Blitz: An Account of Hitler's Aerial War Over Plymouth in March 1941 and the Events that Followed* (Devon Books, 1991).
4   Oral history testimony: Miss L.W., 5 June 2000.
5   Ibid.: Miss E.J., 16 March 1999.
6   Gardiner, J., *The Blitz: The British Under Attack* (2010), p. 313.
7   Garfield, S., *We Are at War* (2005), pp. 50–1.
8   Viscountess Astor speaking to the Supply Committee, Hansard House of Commons Parliamentary Debates, 5th Series, 30 June 1942, vol. 385, col. 122.
9   Oral history interview: D.P., 10 May 2011.
10   Hansard House of Commons Parliamentary Debates, 5th Series, 30 June 1942, vol. 385, col. 121–122.
11   Ibid., col. 82.
12   Hansard House of Commons Parliamentary Debates, 5th Series, 30 June 13942, vol. 385, col. 119.
13   Ibid.

The Birmingham and Coventry Blitz

B irmingham and nearby Coventry were targeted by the Luftwaffe primarily because they represented the hub of British industrial output, small arms manufacturing and aircraft manufacturing. The Spitfire aeroplane factory at Castle Bromwich for instance, was producing around 300 Spitfires and twenty Lancaster bombers a month. This rate of aircraft production far surpassed all other factories across the country. In addition, everything from radio components, vehicle parts, industrial tools, bombs, shell casings, rifles and a variety of other small arms were made in the region. For this reason alone, Birmingham was the second-most heavily bombed city in Britain. Well over 2,000 residents lost their lives in the air raids and the number of fatalities in Coventry amounted to over 1,200. Casualty figures vary according to different sources, but they numbered over 9,000 in Birmingham and over 1,000 in the less densely populated city of Coventry. In terms of civilian evacuation the area was officially designated as an evacuation area before the outbreak of war, and many children were shipped off to Worcestershire and Herefordshire before the raids began. However, as was the norm in nearly every city, the majority of children stayed behind to face the wrath of the enemy.

In comparison to many other cities Birmingham possessed a very progressive city council and its members established specialist boarding schools for some children of the Blitz. Many of these were within the city boundaries while others were located in camp schools on the periphery. They were viewed as something of an experiment in many respects, and they were extremely successful in giving the city's children a high level of care, attention and education. One of the teachers explained that her role was often one of a surrogate parent to parents as well as to their children:

> We used to meet with the parents about once a month. Here and there you had to meet perhaps a bit of belligerence, if there was a disagreement about what was going on, or a child had complained, but the general pattern on parents was one of gratitude, being able to let their feelings spill out from them; in a way, as young teachers, we became almost parent to the parents, because of our position with regard to their children and because in a way we knew a part of life differently from the parents, who were under such a stressful state, coming from, you know, bombing and getting to work, worries about their boys who'd gone off into the Forces, their husbands who'd gone into the Forces; again, we were a bit of security to the parents, that we were acting as parents to those young ones, but they could spill out their anxieties [1]

Most of the teachers who were thrown into the specialist boarding schools were young but sympathetic to their charges. More importantly, they were sympathetic to the plight of thousands of youngsters left homeless by the devastating air raids:

> The situations in Birmingham could be very stressful; children who were living in shelters, or just under one of those beds, big metal things, were living in close proximity to disease and infection. Apart from not having any water, and being surrounded by some of the horrors of the bombing that they may see. So it was – very much a specialist boarding school, which gave its own security, I think, to the children, and certainly opened the eyes of teachers to the background the children came from, but even then it was a special background because of the war years; it didn't reflect the normal life, perhaps, of the children. So that really I think, as a young teacher then of twenty two, which might sound old in the world now, there was a great process of education, knowledge and personal contact, which would not have arisen before the war. You see, you knew the child,

141

you knew she'd made a card for her mum for instance, and you knew that particular child had had a letter and had got a link with home. Whereas another child, you know, poor devil, never had a visitor, never had any letters, wasn't very well dressed; you knew that, close, because you knew that child's face when the other child was getting the letters, you knew that perhaps an outburst of temper, and you knew why there was an outburst of temper, because that child was feeling so much more isolated. And seeing other children, so much more loved, so much more cared for, so that when you were helping that child with a bit of work in any way, it couldn't but temper, say, what might have been your crossness about a standard of something done, you wouldn't do it in the same way. Because you'd got to know that child, and that child's place in life, and you wouldn't use your tongue, perhaps, in the same way as you would to a child who jolly well ought to be able to come to terms with what she had been told to do and could very well do, you see, because you had got to know so much more of the child in the classroom.[2]

The views of adults who spent their childhoods in such specialist schools near Birmingham were positive, and they had warmed to the new and experimental curriculum that encouraged an education that involved community activities. One woman recalled that everything on the curriculum seemed to make sense because it was related to everyday life:

For Geography we'd go to a local farm and learn about crop rotation, haymaking and types of corn. History lessons were based on the local church, and if it was a Norman church then we would learn about the Normans. I would go home to visit sometimes but it was nicer and more fun to be at school. We had picnics down by the river and we paddled and had lots of treats. The Royal Air Force was on Cannock Chase and they gave us concerts. We had films in the evening, sing songs and games. I was rabbit monitor but I did not help with the bee keeping because I was frightened of being stung. I was upset one day because I was told that I had to kill a rabbit so it could be used in a stew for our dinner. I couldn't do it so a teacher had to come and kill it. We each had our own gardening plot and I remember growing radishes and lettuces to give to my parents when they visited. This was separate from the main school garden that was used to grow things for our kitchen. The school seemed to be more like a family because everything was shared and it was less formal than my previous school. I didn't have time to be homesick because there was always something to do.[3]

Within the new specialist boarding schools however, some equipment was limited and teachers were required to work all hours of the day and night. One staff member explained the set up as follows:

We had to work weekends and nights as well as during the day. We actually only taught for half a day. There were two teachers to each class, but they were different children to those in your dormitory. Your dormitory was a mixture of all ages, so we would have the first year children from all over the site. We did have a science laboratory and a home economics laboratory, very rough and ready, but I mean, there were things that the children could learn to cook with, and for the first time, art, which was my subject, could be more specialised. And of course, there we were out of doors. For the very first time I was wandering around with classes of children, and because we were a very new thing in Birmingham there was only a certain amount of money.

In Birmingham, we could see Coventry being burned from where we were; and sometimes the planes would be going over to Liverpool, so we seemed quite often to be under heavy aircraft going across. We had to make plans for what we were to do with the children. The first thing was, children on the top beds getting into the bottom beds, so at least if it came down above you, they were protected by the top bed from anything falling down like that. We were given other choices too. They had cleared some of the ditches, and we were given the choice of either having our children in the bottom beds or taking them out to the ditches. The decision was left to the dormitory mistress. Then we developed a warning system and the deputy head would ride round and round the quad on her bike blowing a whistle, and that was the sign. The first time we did it, I know, we took our children up the road and got into a ditch, and we were the only dormitory that did it. I think that's when we realised that maybe to begin with, it was best for the children to go into the bottom beds.[4]

By November 1940, cities in the Midlands, along with other cities nationwide, had become accustomed to nightly bombing raids. But the night of 14 November remains the most significant date for the residents of Coventry. On this night a total of 449 Luftwaffe bombers targeted the historic city that was largely responsible for the manufacture of munitions, armaments and military vehicles.

A child sheltering with her sister in their nightclothes was driven from under the stairs when their house north-west of the city centre was hit. Running along the street to the public shelter she found:

> although it was November the air was hot and acrid. It was brilliant moonlight and with all the fires it was as bright as day, and the sky was red, just like blood, I remember thinking, and then suddenly I was deadly frightened. And so we ran down that road, which reminded me vividly of a film I had seen, The Last Days of Pompeii, with the buildings on fire and dropping into the road as we ran. It seemed we ran miles and miles until we got to the public shelter, which was crammed with people who were packed further in to make room for us. Children were crying and screaming, women were weeping, and everybody was scared stiff.[5]

The air raid destroyed most of the city and killed over 1,000 of its residents in one night. The spiritual heart of the city had also been ripped out, as the once-beautiful, historic Coventry Cathedral now lay in ruins. For the people of Coventry this was an extremely bitter blow, and one that reverberated throughout its community. Their neighbouring residents in Birmingham had looked on in horror as the bombs had rained down on Coventry and they sent fire crews and medical teams to their aid. The following morning bewildered people gradually came to terms with the immense destruction, and this particular raid on Coventry has since been acknowledged as one of the most devastating raids of the entire war. Over 500 tons of high-explosive bombs had been dropped on the city in one night, and 30,000 incendiary devices. Coventry residents spent the following grim weeks attending mass funerals for their families and neighbours. But the raid did not damage morale in the way that Hitler had expected. Most of them acknowledged that since there was nothing left standing to bomb, they did not need to fear future raids. Moreover the ruins and rubble of Coventry Cathedral became a symbol that served to further unite the British people against the enemy and strengthen their resolve.

The increase in bombing however, did take its toll on the children of Birmingham and Coventry. Consequently, within the specialist schools teachers and pupils began to form unprecedented emotional connections:

Within the dormitory situation, we were as a parent or nurse to a child. Incidentally, we did have our own nurse and our own little hospital on the premises – we had to because of the state of Birmingham at that time. We also had to keep a close watch on vermin and scabies within the dormitory pattern; we'd have the morning teaching, we would have our lunch, then we would all go down and the children would rest on their beds. One teacher would be sitting, and the other two teachers would be sitting in the middle. Children all on their beds, they could nap, or they could read a book, but we had to use that time to inspect their heads. Where of course they were infested we had to cleanse their heads, and this was a daily thing. If you imagine that every day your midday duty was checking or dealing with verminous heads. Although not all of the children were verminous. You also had to cope with the bed wetting. There were some children of course, who just because of circumstances and separation perhaps became bed wetters when they hadn't been before. So you had a very strong emotional programme, a difficulty there. And the child who wet their bed became very smelly and you had to deal with the reactions of the other children. We also had some children who were thieves. But all the problems were met within one situation, so this was happening as though it was happening within your own family. But you had to watch out; I can think of one girl, I won't mention her name, but she wasn't a very pleasant sort of character and she was a terrible thief. Now it was very hard giving her security and watching out to see what she was getting up to, and dealing with what the children thought of her, and all of this was contained in one school. Both the children and teachers were adapting to living a life that brought us much closer together, out of the classroom as well as in, and in a world that concerned us all. So it was a natural thing for barriers to come down. I mean, if a child had lost an uncle, or if a teacher had lost a boyfriend out there in battle, there was a natural concern. As you got together in evening times and other times, there was a closeness that existed between teachers and pupils that did not occur in ordinary schools.[6]

However, not all children were fortunate to be included in the specialist boarding schools and other pupils faced a lottery in terms of their education. One woman, as a child, discovered that she was rendered temporarily deaf when a bomb exploded in a garden near her family's Anderson shelter during an intense air raid:

> I remember the earth shattering sound of the bomb but then I could not hear anything at all for over three weeks. I was very frightened because I could see people's mouths moving but no sound was coming out. I went into school but my teacher thought I was just being naughty when I did not respond to her questions, so I was punished and sent to stand in a corner for hours on end. I didn't know what to do I was only six years old and deaf. I didn't know why. When my hearing returned it came back in spurts of sound, it took ages for everything to sound normal again. I will never forget my teacher's lack of sympathy and understanding, never.[7]

During the war finding suitable teachers presented problems for local education authorities, and school log books reveal that while most teachers went out of their way to help their pupils there were also a number who appeared to possess a sadistic streak. With so many men away at the front older teachers were brought out of retirement to fill the gap; naturally many were none too impressed by this process and a certain amount of irritability found its way into the classrooms. The hitherto organised system of education was reduced to a state of shambles, yet this was not surprising since most city schools were doubling up in terms of the pupil numbers because of bombed-out buildings. Perhaps what is more surprising is the fact that education continued despite the bombing. Most children went to school either in the morning or the afternoon, since there was no room to accommodate all children for the whole day in existing school buildings. This shift system was also prevalent in rural areas where large numbers of evacuees had flooded small village schools. Furthermore, in the specialist schools established by the Birmingham Education Authority, teachers were responsible for pupils throughout the year with little or no respite:

> You see, we had to keep the children over Easter and Christmas, summer holidays too. If it was summertime we used to have sing songs in the evening and a bit of an extra walk or something. We used to organise

a sports games and races, you know, things like that. The men from the Royal Air Force used to come and entertain the children so we had a link with men in the Forces. We were aware of the war and the men and the fronts and things, and of course I particularly was, because I came from Canterbury originally and I was fully aware of the Battle of Britain.[8]

The fact that children in Birmingham, Coventry and other cities were often entertained by members of the armed forces has frequently been overlooked. Indeed, much has been made of people who entertained the troops on the front lines, but little of those in the forces who entertained the folks on the home front. Yet this process of providing children with entertainment was just one of the ways in which military personnel helped to shore up civilian morale. Furthermore, this was a voluntary endeavour, and members of the armed forces became adept at putting on magic shows and variety acts during their off-duty periods; not forgetting the all important pantomimes for the children around Christmas time.

Virtually all teachers who worked during the Blitz and the children who attended their schools remembered the concerts put on by the forces. Regardless of the bombs, rationing and other impositions inflicted by the circumstances of war, adults and children still tried to live their lives as normal in defiance of the enemy. It is fitting, therefore, that Birmingham's most recent memorial to those who were killed in the air raids is a sculpture entitled The Tree of Life. Situated in Edgbaston Street, next to St Martins Church in the Bullring, the 12ft 6in sculpture contains the names of all those who died (whose names are known). The tree itself emerges from the ground, and is surmounted by two hands signifying people coming together.[9]

Notes

1   Oral history testimony: Miss M.S.J., 27 July 1998. University of Cambridge 'Teaching in Wartime' project respondent no. 007.

2   Ibid.

3   Oral history testimony; Mrs A.S.R., 5 July 2000.

4   Ibid.: Miss M.S.J., 27 July 1998. University of Cambridge 'Teaching in Wartime' project respondent no. 007.

5   Gardiner, J., *The Blitz: The British Under Attack* (2010), p. 145.

6   Ibid.

7   Oral history testimony: Miss O.S., 10 July 2001.

8   Ibid.: Miss A.S.R., 27 July 1998.

9   Information obtained from the Birmingham Blitz Remembered website: http://www.bbc.co.uk/birmingham/content/articles/2005/10/04/memorial_feature.shtml.

12

The London Blitz

As the nation's capital city and seat of government, London was obviously a prime target for enemy action and was therefore designated an evacuation area by the Anderson Committee. Moreover it was the East End docklands and surrounding areas that bore the brunt of London's Blitz, which began on 7 September 1940. London also suffered more than any other city from what became known as the 'baby Blitz'. This was the period when Hitler attacked the capital and southern England with V-1 and V-2 rockets. These pilot-less monoplanes became known as the flying bombs or Doodlebugs, and began to hit London in mid-June 1944. They were frequently launched in daylight and could not be detected by radar. Carrying a 1 ton warhead, the V-1 travelled at 350mph to a preset target. From 1944 onwards, 9,521 V-1 rockets were fired on London and the south. Anti-aircraft fire and Royal Air Force fighters destroyed 4,621 of these. The later V-2 rockets were faster and more difficult to destroy, since they could travel at supersonic speed; around 5,000 of these rockets were aimed specifically at London. Furthermore, the Doodlebugs were viewed as more sinister and alarming by Londoners than the earlier heavy bombing Blitz, because there was no warning of their arrival and, therefore, no time for anyone to take cover before they exploded. Fortunately many of the V-2 rockets experienced mechanical problems, and due to the speed of impact damage was often inflicted deep underground. Nevertheless, in terms of the Blitz, London undoubtedly suffered more than any other city. The number of civilians killed was 20,000, and 3,000 of these in one night alone. In the worst single incident, 450 were killed when a bomb hit an air-raid shelter at a school in West Ham.[1]

In total there were three main evacuation timelines during which children were taken out of London to places of relative safety. The first major evacuation coincided with that of other British cities and took place from 31 August 1939 over a period of three days immediately prior to the declaration of war. The second was initiated by the Minister of Health 13–18 June 1940 – because intelligence reports suggested that large-scale bombing of London by the enemy was imminent – and the third occurred in 1944 in response to the Doodlebug raids. In addition to these tangible evacuation timelines there was also a constant ebb and flow of children migrating to and from country areas to cities and sometimes back again, seemingly at random. This process was usually dictated by individual family circumstances. For example, many children were abandoned due to the loss of their homes and immediate relatives. This was a social problem that affected the whole country but was particularly acute and more visible in the London area. Voluntary services and local authorities did their best to keep track of such children and provide them with a safety net of care, but this was not always possible. Some children who were often bewildered and panic stricken as a result of the bombing, invariably slipped through the net and wandered the streets for days on end. Yet amongst the stories of sorrow and distress there were also stories of dramatic survival, as when a three-week-old baby girl was discovered buried under a mountain of rubble and lying in the arms of her dead grandmother after a period of three days. Moreover, the intensity of the Blitz prompted many mothers to reconsider their earlier decision to stay in London and a large number of them made desperate attempts to flee the city.

Councillor Frank R. Lewey, Lord Mayor of Stepney in London's East End, described the aftermath of one bombing raid as follows:

We resolved to occupy the People's Palace, the Theatre in the Mile End Road ... this place was big enough to give us elbow room in handling the masses of homeless who were already tramping in like a retreating army, seeking our assistance ... When we first set up business at the People's Palace ... our very first task was to arrange for the evacuation of mothers and small children who had been rendered homeless, and, after those, for the mothers and children who wished to leave London. I myself, dog tired after a terrific days work, dragging wearily out of the People's Palace and seeing in front of me a great area of deserted prams in the evening

light, with the drifting smoke of nearby burning houses dimming them
… The mothers had brought their babies in prams, and, of course, we
had not foreseen that, and, as they could not take the prams with them on
the overcrowded trains, they just had to leave them there in front of the
building, so that it was by evening, hardly possible to get in or out except
by climbing over a great expanse of them.[2]

However, in a similar scenario to the 1939 evacuation the numbers of evacuated
children in 1940 still fell short of government expectations. Indeed, around
25 per cent of children whose parents had registered them under the new scheme
failed to turn up for the trains that were designated to take them to the country.
Mothers had simply changed their minds about sending their children away.
By means of propaganda government officials had achieved limited success
in terms of persuading parents to leave existing evacuees in the country, but
evacuee host family conflicts continued to hamper their efforts in this respect.
Most London mothers, therefore, with a sense of gritty determination, decided
to ride out the Blitz rather than escape to the country. For some this decision
rested on a stubborn refusal to let the enemy force them out of their homes, for
others it was a matter of necessity to stay put. Many women wanted to work and
had other family commitments, such as elderly relatives to care for, or children
with sickness or disabilities. When trying to help these mothers government
ministers were often at odds when deciding the best course of action. A wave
of national publicity also highlighted the advantages and disadvantages of
various policy decisions with regard to the care of London's children. It seemed
that everyone had an opinion as to how the government should proceed. This
publicity naturally prompted numerous debates in the House of Commons, and
Mr Willink outlined his assessment of the issue to the Supply Committee:

I was asked if I would keep an eye on the provision and arrangements for
nurseries in the London region. Since then I have seen a good deal of it,
and in these circumstances the observations I shall offer to the Committee
will be of an objective and factual, and not an argumentative, character
and I hope may prove of some little interest.

I found this task most puzzling when I started to look at it, because the
whole policy in full of apparent contradictions. In the first place, there
was nothing more painful than to find children under five in certain parts

of central London. On the other hand, large numbers of children under this age were there, and their mothers were desirous of working. The next one – and one to which I found an echo in my heart – was that medical officers of health did not like to see very young babies being put into these nurseries and their mothers going to work. Still, their mothers were going to work or desirous of working, either for economic, or more frequently for patriotic, reasons. Consequently, there was for this great Metropolitan area a need to be met. I found in the nature of things that it was extremely difficult to find proper accommodation in many areas. Only gradually are we getting those straight and extracting nursery schools from the National Fire Service and the Civil Defence Services, and in other ways. Local authorities proceed at very different rates. When I began to look into this question I found that there were twenty five nurseries open in the London region and forty two schemes approved. Now I am glad to say that in five months those figures have risen to one hundred and twenty nine nurseries open and seventy one more approved. In addition to these two classes, open or approved, at the earlier date there were and at the present date there are eighty or ninety further schemes in preparation.[3]

In the same speech Mr Willink also made it clear that the rapid expansion of nursery places in London did not constitute a long-term policy goal with regard to children under 5:

Frankly, I approach this matter as a wartime measure. It is not part of the general development schemes for the welfare of young children. Its purpose is to make the very best provision which will give facilities and confidence to mothers who desire to work in national industry. On that basis, what one does, of course, is to keep in the closest touch with the Ministry of Labour. Those who do the detailed work are in daily, if not more than daily, touch with the Minister of Labour as to where nurseries should be opened.[4]

In essence, government ministers were caught in a catch twenty-two situation. Ideally they wanted all children to be evacuated out of London for safety reasons, this would then free up mothers to work in munitions and other war-related production work. They were also deeply aware that all child guidance and medical advice stated that children under the age of 5 should be kept with their mothers. If all of these mothers had left London with their little ones, however, there would be severe labour shortages and the war effort would suffer. Given this scenario, and the fact that many mothers felt duty bound by a sense of patriotism to assist the war effort, ministers had little choice but to provide as many nurseries as possible. Evidence also reveals that a distinct lack of suitable billets in the country also restricted the ability of mothers to leave the city with their children. On one night, for instance, Oxford was swamped by over 6,000 fleeing Londoners looking for a bed. The local authority was forced to commandeer the Majestic Cinema in order to house them all. Somewhat ironically under the circumstances, the cinema was screening *Babes in the Wood*.[5]

Nevertheless, with their men away fighting at the front most women, including mothers, felt the necessity to make some contribution to the war effort. As the war progressed the Ministry of Labour was given powers to direct some women into factories and areas where they were most needed, but mothers with small children were left to choose their own war work. Nurseries were duly built as close to the work place as possible, and this enabled mothers to deposit and collect their children with ease as they walked to and from work. But the sheer level of bombing took its toll on Londoners and their children. In one period, for example, between 7 September and 2 November 1941, London was bombed every single night and sometimes during the day. One gentleman remembers the Blitz with vivid clarity, and details the difficult choices people were faced with:

I recall one night in particular when the bombing was horrendous, completely terrifying. I was only eight years old at the time and when the siren went my mother rushed us all into an underground air raid shelter. It was somewhere near some arches, near the Tate and Lyle sugar factory in the East End. At any rate, we all huddled together, held hands and tried to sing as loudly as we could. It seemed as though the bombing would never stop and the grown-ups looked very frightened, even though they were putting on a brave face for us children. After a while an A.R.P. man came down to the shelter and told us that there was an unexploded bomb right above our heads. He said we had a choice of whether to go out of the shelter or stay where we were. He then told us that there was so much shrapnel flying about that we were more likely to be injured by shrapnel than by the bomb. Anyway, there was some whispered discussion amongst the grown-ups and they decided that we would take our chances and stay put. Thankfully the bomb didn't go off and it was probably dealt with the next day.[6]

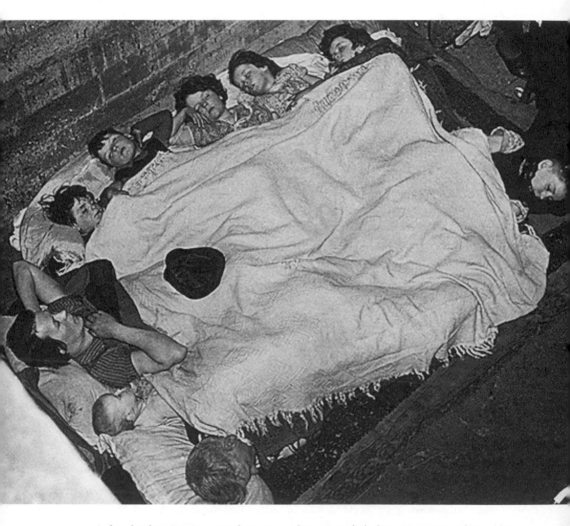

A family sleeping in a south-east London air-raid shelter. (Courtesy of Franklin D. Roosevelt image library)

This unexploded bomb constituted just one of around 3,000 that were successfully dealt with by bomb disposal experts during London's Blitz, and over 200,000 Air Raid Precaution wardens helped to defend the city. These wardens were assisted by firewatchers, many of whom were young teenagers. Such was the ferocity and intensity of the London Blitz that the war organisation of the British Red Cross and the Order of St John established a rest house scheme for civil defence workers. These included well-supervised nurseries for children, but they were not always appreciated by members of the wider public. Indeed there were some who poured scorn on the whole project since:

> An impression arose that it was a way of providing free holidays for a class of hale and hearty civilians who were subjected to no greater strain than others in civil life – a view disputed by Lord Horder, who described the scheme as a piece of pioneering work in preventative medicine.[7]

The rest house schemes were viewed as an experiment, but they were such a success in terms of giving civil defence workers and their children some much-needed respite from the continual strain of defending the city during air raids that they were copied by council officials. In fact, it appears that some Members of Parliament believed the experiment to have been initiated by councillors rather than the voluntary workers of the Red Cross and St John. As Mr Willink propounded in 1942:

> I should like to mention one or two experiments we have been making. In the county of London, the Metropolitan Boroughs are the maternity and child welfare authorities, but the London County Council has been offering their assistance, and one experiment is already well established and another is coming along. One result of the heavy bombing was that a year ago London had a large number of equipped rest centres with staff, and it has been most desirable in periods of lull that the staff should be used. I am glad to say that there are twenty projects, twelve of which are completely in operation, of wartime nurseries in the rest centres. Those nurseries are only for children between two and five because there is not any special staff ... This policy would have gone much further but for the difficulty of accommodation in the London area.[8]

The combination of voluntary and official council efforts did much to alleviate the suffering of Londoners and their children. There is also plenty of evidence to support the notion that children helped to shore up adult morale. As Hitler's bombs pounded the nation's capital night after night, the presence of children actually contributed to the British bulldog spirit of resistance. As families pulled together it is clear that the laughter, acceptance and humour of children helped to maintain morale. According to the Home Intelligence Service, public morale was dependent on several factors, including the provision of hot food, a safe haven and a good sleep.

It was also important for people to recognise that the burdens associated with war deprivations and the quality of sacrifices were shared across classes. Morale was inextricably linked to an unfailing trust in Britain's national leadership and an unwavering belief in eventual victory. In this sense, it was undoubtedly Churchill's riveting and uplifting speeches that fortified the nation.[9] Arguably, children played a significant role in morale building, since they reminded people of their nation's future and their existence on city streets represented a positive visual sign that the enemy had not defeated British society, nor had he beaten the British people into submission. As one observer noted: 'The sight and sound of children playing on city streets seemed like an act of defiance, it was normality flying in the face of the abnormal.'[10]

Adults naturally felt compelled to make an effort for city children. For instance, Christmas trees were taken down to London's Underground stations and shelters in December 1940, where they were decorated lovingly and attentively in much the same way as they had been in people's own homes. Children even put out their stockings for Father Christmas on Christmas Eve. Choirs of adults and children sang Christmas carols and held hands as the bombs rained down overhead.

It was wonderful to see kids – some of them homeless and some of them orphans – enjoying themselves. Christmas trees were erected in ticket halls and decorated with stashes of pre-war ornaments – tinsel, baubles, paper lanterns, balloons, miniature crackers, sometimes fairy lights and, invariably, a celluloid fairy/doll/angel with a white crepe paper dress at the top. Paper chains were strung along the platforms and some 11,000 toys were distributed to 'Underground children.' The Swiss Cottager announced that £4 10s had been collected from among the shelterers for a Christmas party for the children sleeping in the station.

Flo Robinson travelled by tube from the East End to Paddington, from where she took a train to spend Christmas in Taunton, Somerset:

All the stations had parties going on. I've never seen so many Christmas trees in one night. Each platform had one at each end; there were accordions, banjos, trumpets, anything on which to play a tune, singing, dancing and even a Santa Claus. It was lovely to see how Londoners really knew how to make the most of a rough situation.[11]

In the mornings following an air raid, Londoners would emerge weary but relieved from their Underground refuge, and most would immediately look for the outline of St Paul's Cathedral on the horizon. For the vast majority of Londoners this particular building, along with that of Westminster Abbey, represented the religious spirit of the capital and was viewed as crucial for morale. People were also very quick to establish a sense of order after air raids, as a BBC reporter surveying the damage of the Blitz noted.

The streets have all been instantly and neatly swept, so that there is no look of demoralisation. The broken glass is all in tidy piles. Men go down the street sweeping it up into gutters as if it were ice. The roping off is as firm as the roping off of a boxing ring. You stare at the wreck of a house or a roped round crater in the road, and, wanton as the damage is, you do feel as though somebody has already taken charge. London was never as efficient during peace time.[12]

In the early stages of war some government officials had voiced misgivings about the safety of sheltering in the Underground railway stations and had even barred the entrances to many of them. Londoners, however, took matters into their own hands and simply bought train tickets, went underground and stayed there. Prime Minister Winston Churchill sensibly agreed with ordinary Londoners that such stations provided the best shelters possible, despite the appalling incident at Bank station. Subsequently, much of the London population inhabited the Underground for the duration of the war, and their response to the Blitz in terms of organising food, health and entertainment in the Underground stations was a wonder to behold. In total, seventy-nine Underground tube stations were used as havens from enemy bombardment, and it was not uncommon for troops to take refuge in the tube stations as they moved across London. Government and voluntary organisations improved the lighting and toilet amenities, and food, drinks, entertainment and bedding were provided when necessary. Some individuals even chalked out their territory on station platforms. Furthermore, most children appreciated the safe but subterranean environment of London's Underground system:

> Sometimes you could hear the bombs going off and other times you didn't but it didn't seem to matter. What mattered was that I was with my family. We held hands, sang songs and told each other jokes until the all clear sounded. Well, you couldn't do that with strangers now, could you?[13]

Even children who had been evacuated from London often ran away from their host families in order to get back to their beloved city. Sometimes these flights were prompted by homesickness and a longing to be reunited with parents, sometimes by the desire to escape unhappy billets. Many became adept at fooling adults along the way. For example, as a child, Claire Rayner ran away from host families on a regular basis in order to get back to her home in London and was well used to using guile:

> I developed a technique I suppose you could call it, for not being noticed as a runaway. I would attach myself to a friendly looking person, usually a woman on her own but sometimes a couple, and say in a vague but unworried fashion that my mother and three sisters were further up the train and that I'd come down to this end to see if there were any seats. But of course there weren't. There never were. I would perch on the nearest piece of luggage and chatter to them in a cheerful sort of fashion until they were used to me being there. After a while I would say I was going back to the other end to see if my mother and sisters had found seats and set off to push my way through the unbelievably crowded corridors to the other end.
>
> I learned early on these journeys to listen out for the cry, 'Tickets Please! If you please. Tickets! Tickets per-lease', of the ticket inspector. At this stage the railways still tried to use them on their trains; later they gave up in despair, for completing the job of inspecting a train full of tickets in those conditions had to be hell on earth. But as soon as I heard the cry

I would head for the lavatory. Even if there was someone in it, they were usually out of it by the time the inspector got to me; if they were tardy I'd bang on the door and plead urgency. It usually worked. The trick then was to leave the lavatory unlocked, and press myself against the wall behind the door, alongside the pan. The inspector would push it open as he went by to make sure he missed no passengers, but he didn't push it all the way so he didn't find me. The excitement of tricking my way back to London had been wonderful, but once I arrived I thought of my mother. I had to go home to her. There was nowhere else. I knew she would beat me. I knew after the first time she did it that she would probably arrange to have me sent away again. But still I did it. Why? Because it was better than my evacuee life.[14]

The exact number of runaways is not known, though a survey of school log books reporting incidents of children absconding from reception areas indicates that other children were replicating Claire Rayner's strategy and finding their own way back to the cities by devious means. This situation added to the problem of providing adequate care for children. But, surprisingly, there was more sympathy for mothers who had chosen to keep their children in the cities than one might have expected given the circumstances. A secretary named Pam Ashford living in blitzed Clydeside, Scotland, wrote in her diary with regard to the bombing of London:

People are, of course, looking at pictures in the newspapers closely and expressing such sentiments as, 'London has had a bad time!' If the raid was meant to appal the British nation it has completely failed as far as Clydeside is concerned. I said, 'I wonder what people who kept their children in London think now!' expecting everyone would say, 'Now they will wish they took the Government's advice,' which is my way of thinking. I was surprised to find Agnes saying, 'They will be glad they kept them at home. If your house is bombed you will want your children with you.' Miss Smith: 'It must be terrible to think that if you are killed your children are with strangers in the country.' There was a general agreement that country people don't want evacuees, excepting Guernsey children who are reported to be nicely mannered.[15]

Whilst others around the country looked on in horror at the bombing of civilian targets (such as London's maternity hospital), ordinary Londoners found heroic sides to their nature as they rescued countless adults and children from the wrecks and rubble caused by the nightly onslaughts. Older children helped to clean up the streets, run errands and assist rescuers in their noble attempts to save lives amidst the destruction. It is also important to recognise that the perception of childhood was very different in the 1930s and '40s. The majority of children left school at the age of 14 and were quickly absorbed into the adult workplace and adult environments.

Although it was acknowledged that children of 14 years should not be allowed to fight, in terms of the war effort they were nevertheless brought into the civil defence services and the light rescue teams. As members of these teams they were taught how to reconnect electricity cables, turn off power supplies, put out fires that were started by incendiary bombs, use resuscitation techniques when necessary and administer first aid. They acted as police messengers, firewatchers and stretcher bearers, and were often used to carry telegrams that carried news to families of those missing in action. Originally young boys were given the task of delivering messages to and from various rescue workers, engineers and families.

Even a small bombing raid would result in the disruption of services, including the telephone service. Underground cables and pipes would be severed, telegraph poles brought down and, in some cases, exchanges hit. In these eventualities messages would have to be sent by a system of runners or messengers. At first these messengers were part of the different services; wardens' messengers were usually chosen from local youth groups such as the Boy Scouts or Boys' Brigade, but soon after the start of the war the government became concerned about the possible casualties amongst youngsters and directed authorities to replace them with older volunteers, usually between the ages of 15 and 18. Younger volunteers, known as 'young citizens', were used as messengers in post-raid work and formed into pools usually based in schools, called the Aftermath Messenger Service.[16]

In terms of the children's war effort in London and nationwide it was the Boy Scouts and Girl Guides that provided the backbone of child labour. These Christian voluntary organisations founded by Lord Baden-Powell continued to provide children with a practical skills base and an education long after they left school. Certainly the majority of evacuees worked on the land, while city children worked in factories and shops, but the children who belonged to the Girl Guide and Boy Scout movements were fundamental to the war effort. Their organisational network stretched across the country and their common sense practical skills were a valuable resource.

The Girl Guides, for instance, were commissioned by the Ministry of Food to teach 'Blitz cooking' to Londoners who had been bombed out of their homes. This involved teaching women how to emerge from bombsites and make emergency ovens out of bricks, and how to cook makeshift nutritious meals in such ovens once they were constructed. They also helped to distribute gas masks, painted pavement kerbs white to guide people in the black out, kept up morale by singing in the air-raid shelters and raised money in order to buy ambulances and life boats. Although Girl Guides did indulge in the more stereotypically female occupations such as knitting socks and scarves for soldiers, their training techniques encompassed a broad range of skills. For instance, Guides were earning proficiency badges in work fields such as mechanics, plumbing, electrical wiring, first aid and telegraphic communications. The latter demanded that girls built their own wireless receivers; they were also required to transmit Morse Code messages at the rate of thirty per minute. In the country they were often responsible for organising evacuees and digging for victory campaigns, while in the cities they were busy helping to run nurseries, assisting with food supplies, making emergency shelters, administering first aid and teaching practical skills. Moreover, the Guiding movement arguably did much to remove class barriers, since girls from all ages and all backgrounds were involved in the organisation.[17]

The same was true of the Scouting movement, who were involved in numerous activities during the war. Adopting the slogan 'Boy Scouts are Carrying On', there were 53,000 scouts trained to undertake over 170 National War Service jobs by the end of 1940.[18] As faith-based organisations, the Guides and the Scouts were fundamental in terms of maintaining morale and they were instructed by their leaders to do their duties with cheerfulness and selflessness. A sense of duty to God, monarch and country, strength of character, self-reliance and a determination to help others were – and still are – key features of these youth movements. Plentiful examples of bravery on the part of children involved in the Guides and Scouts during the war were outward manifestations of the underpinning ethos of these organisations.

Frank Davis, for instance, was a member of the 11th Bermondsey and Rotherhithe (St James) Group who, at the tender age of 17, died while rescuing a fellow Scout at Trinity Church Dockhead, London, on 8 December 1940. He was awarded the Bronze Cross for conspicuous bravery and devotion to duty. Self-sacrificing valour in Boy Scouts was inspired by strong, forthright and courageous leadership, such as that provided by patrol leader George Collins, Sea Scout of the 12th Shoreditch (Jubilee) Group. The *Weekly News* reported his selfless act of courage as follows:

> He was in a street in which two houses were struck during an enemy air raid on 8th October 1940. Running to the spot he discovered that in one house there had been three children in bed on the first floor. No one knew whether the children were still there and Collins volunteered to find out. No ladders were available and the stairs and half the lower part of the house had been blown away, so he climbed over the debris and with great difficulty, reached the bedroom in which the children were trapped. He had to dig with his hands through about three feet of rubble and plaster but managed to get the injured children out safely and pass them down to helpers outside. Throughout this action Collins was in grave danger since the floor of the bedroom was gradually giving way and the outside wall was liable to crumble at any moment, but he refused to come down until his task was finished, despite the enemy planes overhead.[19]

George Collins was awarded a Silver Cross for his noble actions, and similar dramatic rescues were performed by Scouts across the country. As children were prone to follow the examples set by adults the philosophy of thinking of others first and foremost permeated British culture during the Blitz. People had very little in the way of belongings, but a community spirit evolved that cemented human relationships. It was quite usual, for example, to find four families living together in one house, simply because people were losing their homes on a nightly basis. Relatives and neighbours rallied round to help each other in the face of a common enemy. Older children who remained in London became part of the civil defence teams that fought to save the city, and they were proud to have played that part. As a gentleman who had been a young firefighter during the Blitz recalled: 'All childhood things had gone but I felt a part of saving London.'[20]

The London Blitz

London children in Blitz conditions grew up quickly and adopted a sense of responsibility at an early age, none more so than the young Princess Elizabeth, who gave her first BBC broadcast, addressing the nation's children at home and abroad, during the dark days of the Blitz on 13 October 1940:

In wishing you all Good evening I feel that I am speaking to friends and companions who have shared with my sister and myself many a happy Children's Hour. Thousands of you in this country have had to leave your homes and be separated from your fathers and mothers. My sister Margaret Rose, and I feel so much for you, as we know from experience what it means to be away from those we love most of all. To you, living in new surroundings, we send a message of true sympathy, and at the same time we would like to thank all the kind people who have welcomed you to their homes in the country.

All of us children who are still at home think continually of our friends and relations who have gone overseas who have travelled thousands of miles to find a new wartime home and a kindly welcome in Canada, Australia, New Zealand, South Africa and the United States of America. My sister and I feel that we know quite a lot about these countries. Our father and mother have so often talked to us of their visits to different parts of the world. So it is not difficult for us to picture the sort of life you are all leading, and to think of all the new sights you must be seeing and the adventures you must be having. But I am sure that you too are often thinking of the Old Country I know you won't forget us; it is just because we are not forgetting you that I want, on behalf of all the children at home, to send you our love and best wishes to you and your kind hosts as well.

Before I finish, I can truthfully say to you all that we children at home are full of cheerfulness and courage. We are trying to do all we can to help our gallant sailors, soldiers and airmen, and we are trying too, to bear our own share of the danger and sadness of war. We know everyone of us, that in the end all will be well; for God will care for us and give us victory and peace. And when peace comes, remember it will be for us, the children of today, to make the world of tomorrow a better and happier place.[21]

City children across the country were uplifted by this royal speech and British children everywhere responded positively to the young princess and her sister by writing letters of thanks and sending them good wishes. But London was the home of the current and future monarch and it was arguably London's children who listened more acutely to the royal speech. They suffered more than any other group of children at the hands of enemy bombers, yet a large majority of them fought hard and long to save the capital for future generations. It was with some satisfaction, therefore, that the official Home Intelligence Service reported that the morale of Londoners and their children throughout the war was beyond praise.

Notes

1   Facts and figures obtained from Wheal, E.A., Pope, S. and Robbins, K., *The Macmillan Dictionary of the Second World War* (1995). Please also see www.museumoflondon.org.uk/archive/exhibits/blitz/bigstory.html.

2   Inglis, R., *The Children's War* (1989), p. 77.

3   Hansard House of Commons Parliamentary Debates, 5th Series, Report of the Supply Committee, 30 June 1942, vol. 385, col. 115.

4   Ibid., col. 116.

5   Holman, B., *Evacuation: A Very British Revolution* (1995), p. 48.

6   Oral history testimony: E.A.S., 22 June 2011.

7   Cambray, P.G. and Briggs, G.G.B., *The Official History of the British Red Cross and the Order of St John* (1949), p. 416.

8   Hansard House of Commons Parliamentary Debates, 5th Series, 30 June 1942, vol. 385, col.118.

9   Humphries, S., *Secrets of the Blitz*, Testimony Film Productions, first broadcast 22 January 2011.

10 Oral history testimony: Granger, C., August 2008.

11 Gardiner, J., *The Blitz: The British Under Attack* (2010), p. 227

12 Clemence Dane, BBC Overseas Service broadcast, 24 September 1940.

13 Oral history testimony: E.A.S., 22 June 2011.

14 Rayner, C., *How Did I Get Here From There?* (2003), pp. 64–5.

15 Garfield, S., *We Are At War* (2005), p. 362.

16 Brown, M., *Put That Light Out! Britain's Civil Defence Services At War 1939–1945*, p. 36.

17 Cherryman, B., 'How the Girl Guides Knitted, Nursed and Dug for Victory' in *BBC News Magazine*, 30 August 2010, review of Hampton, J., *How Girl Guides Won the War*.

18 The Scout Association Archive. For further information, please see www.scoutsrecords.org.

19 Ibid.

20 Holsgrove, R., speaking in the documentary produced by Humphries, S., *Secrets of the Blitz*, Testimony Film Productions, broadcast 22 January 2011.

21 Her Royal Majesty Queen Elizabeth II addressing British children on BBC radio, 13 October 1940.

13

The Moral Crusade

While government officials and voluntary organisations did their best to safeguard the physical health and welfare of children on a daily basis – with varying degrees of success – there was another group of individuals and authorities that attempted to provide and safeguard their spiritual welfare. This was much easier said than done. Contemporary surveys and reports pertaining to children were not merely concerned with ongoing dilemmas about accommodation, cultural changes, emotional separations and social upheaval, they were also full of religious concerns for the souls of children.

For instance, Roman Catholic priests in Liverpool were convinced beyond any doubt that the children of their congregation who were evacuated to Protestant and Methodist Wales were in severe moral danger. One such priest even advised parents to bring their evacuated children back to the cities despite the bombing, because in his view the German bombs posed a lesser threat than that of moral and spiritual corruption.[1]

From a glance at the Welsh nationalist papers it is also clear that they were not impressed to receive a large number of evacuees who could potentially dilute their congregational religious culture and language. The latter need not have worried however, because English children actually mastered the Welsh language and the feared dilution of religion and culture did not occur. The children left behind in the citie, on the other hand, did not have such acute dilemmas to face in terms of their religious affiliations, since for many of them it was a case of attending whatever church was left standing after the raids!

Surprisingly however, Sunday schools continued to thrive in bombed-out cities, along with other Christian youth groups. Children like Iris Williams, living in Blitz-torn Bristol, even acquired bell-ringing techniques:

> I started bell ringing at St Johns in the arch and we had to learn on muffled bells because we weren't allowed to ring them properly. I attended Sunday school at the Gospel Hall, but I was confirmed at Westbury Church. We children moved around the churches a lot because there was so much bomb damage.[2]

The muffled bell technique was used for all children who wanted to take up the popular pastime of bell ringing, because the actual ringing of church bells during the war would have signalled an invasion. Migration from one church to another was also common as city clergymen put aside denominational differences for the good of their community. Their intimate knowledge of their parish communities was apparent from the time the first enemy bombs were dropped, and they naturally became the first port of call for those who were distressed, made homeless by the bombs or suffering bereavement. It was the clergy who opened their church doors to offer people shelter in the crypts, attended to bomb victims, sorted out administration problems, offered a degree of food and comfort, often co ordinated voluntary organisations and continued to act with dignity and humanity. Father Groser, from London's East End, recorded the vital human kindness and simplicity of these actions by stating that the fact 'we just carried on was of the greatest importance ... a reminder that life and hope endured in the midst of such chaos and uncertainty.'[3]

There was no doubt that churches were on the front line of war in every sense. Blitz conditions were also the strongest test of faith for those who led the nation's religious worship. The newly appointed Rector of Filton Parish Church, Rev. Cecil R. Haslum, recorded the events of the first daylight bombing raids in his diary on 25 September 1940 as follows: 'There was the noise of terrific explosions and falling glass. The Rodney sections of the Aeroplane works was much damaged; many people were killed in the works; many parishioners were injured and some died as their house were wrecked. A terrible day with much sorrow and sadness.'

The bodies of ninety-one dead were brought into the church and the church school. Rev. Haslum spent the day comforting the bereaved, making tea for the mortuary attendants in the church, and visiting the injured in Southmead Infirmary. The following Sunday the Harvest Festival was cancelled and Holy Communion was conducted in the church hall because cleaners were still cleaning the church after the raids. The parish began burying their dead on 2 October. For Rev. Haslum this was a particularly emotional and sorrowful day. To his dismay he found himself conducting the first of many wartime funerals in his new parish, that of a little girl who had been a bridesmaid at the first wedding ceremony he had conducted in there only a fortnight earlier on 21 September.[4]

Upholding and maintaining the faith of the nation under such trying circumstances was a task of enormous importance. The Ministry of Information had recognised that religious belief was an essential component of morale, but trying to instil the love and mercy of Almighty God amidst the suffering and conditions of war was not easy. The following children's Sunday school hymn was etched on city air-raid shelters as a reminder to those who sought shelter:

> God is our refuge, be not afraid.
> He will take care of you through the raid.
> When bombs are dropping and danger near,
> He will be with you, until the all clear.[5]

Yet as people searched for answers and children huddled together nightly in air-raid shelters across the country, they began to question the morality of the war. There was no doubt in the minds of many that tyrannical dictatorships and their lack of respect for the Almighty were the root cause of conflict. Thus a new wave of religious fervour began to take hold of the nation, though the movement had in fact started to take shape even before the bombing began. It was initiated by *The Times* newspaper on 17 February 1940 and was specifically aimed at children and their future moral education. Quickly dubbed the 'new crusade', *The Times* featured a series of articles and statements which lobbied for more Christian teaching in schools. According to these articles the example of Nazi Germany, which had eradicated religious instruction from German schools, provided ample evidence that without Christian values a nation sank into a moral abyss.

Henceforth *The Times*, the Ministry of Information and most religious leaders portrayed the war as a morally just, religious crusade against the dark pagan forces of Nazism. Furthermore, although some scholars have since ridiculed this stance, this view was based on a substantial body of evidence. For instance, it was known for certain that high-ranking Nazi leaders such as Himmler did indulge in pagan rituals with the intention of conjuring up dark forces. Much as they seemed to be ludicrous and nonsensical rituals to members of the normal British public, there was plenty of evidence to suggest that a pagan, godless Nazi society was responsible for a number of evils. When *The Times*, therefore, claimed that British children were in danger of moral decline unless their schooling was solely based on Christian teaching, it did so with the best of intentions and a good deal of public support.

For the best part of 1940 and 1941 the new moral crusade gathered momentum and *The Times* continually advocated for 'a real Christian education system for the children of a Christian land'.[6] Petitions were organised in church parishes and councils, and magazines such as the *Catholic Herald* extolled the importance of fighting secularism. Indeed, Anglican, Roman Catholic and nonconformist groups were all united in their demands for faith-based education. Christian teaching, they argued, was the only way to protect the souls of children. Eventually Lambeth Palace issued a statement which argued for the need for compulsory Christian teaching in all schools. There were also suggestions that teachers, members of local education authorities and school managers should all be tested on their religious convictions. As the Blitz became more intense the moral crusade appeared to adopt a sense of urgency. An article published in February 1941 in the *Journal of Education* claimed: 'The public is now looking for such reforms but will become apathetic again if action be too long delayed: and each year a further batch of semi-pagan children passes from school life into citizenship.'[7]

However, while it was laudable to agitate for a Christian-based education system, it was a bit of an exaggeration to call British schoolchildren semi-pagan. In fact, it could be argued that children were getting more religious instruction than they had hitherto been accustomed to receiving. Although church attendance had fallen because over half the population were away fighting and churches were being bombed in all major cities, religious services were held in Underground shelters, church crypts, people's houses, and school and office buildings. Children, therefore, were in no doubt as to the basics of Christian teachings, and most youth organisations were attached to churches and religious communities.

The new crusade also had its detractors. Many in the teaching profession felt that there was no need to whip up religious fervour against the enemy, and argued that media attention would be better spent on asking for practical help to deal with bombed-out schools, a lack of air-raid shelters and school equipment. In truth, there were very few teachers who objected to the idea of a Christian-based educational system, but they did take exception to proposals that suggested teachers needed to be vetted for evidence of good Christian principles and moral behaviour. A headmaster from Cambridge Heath, for example, wrote to the editor of the *Journal of Education* to protest against such policy:

> Sir – I am one of those (there must be many) who are grateful to your journal for the statesmanlike attitude you have taken in this delicate and difficult matter of religious teaching. Those of us who do not see eye to eye with the ecclesiastical hierarchy are beginning to wonder whether we are to be examined by an inquisition into our religious views and whether we are coming back to the merry sport of frying astronomers. One might almost suppose, in reading the columns of the Times that the works of John Stuart Mill and others had fallen into complete oblivion. The kindly observations of Mr Jenkyn-Thomas embolden me to make my own protest against the New Order now being proposed by many good Christian people, who imagine the comely governance of our lives is impossible except under their special guidance. Their intentions are good. Some of their proposals are infamous.[8]

Another gentleman named Frank Roscoe wrote in a similar vein: 'In these grey days the magnificent silliness of the suggestion gives welcome excuse for mirth.'[9]

Nevertheless, concern for children's spiritual wellbeing continued unabated and gained further prominence in the education debates that led up to the Butler Education Act of 1944. Within these crucial parliamentary debates the views of government ministers were polarised between those who favoured an education system based on science and those who argued for a system based on religion. In addition, education debates also prompted a number of left-wing MPs to call for the abolition of public schools. According to such MPs, the latter schools, along with various youth movements, could be blamed for militarising the nation's youth. In their view, dangerous parallels could be drawn with the mechanistic education system that existed in Germany. Speaking in 1942, one MP declared:

> All youth movements, all the regimentation we are now seeking to impose on our educational system, were there in the Weimar Republic. All Hitler had to do was amalgamate them, to 'trustify' them so to speak. I am desperately afraid that this is happening in this country. It is an English form of totalitarianism, and English form of dragooning and militarising. I do not mean militarising in the sense of using a rifle; I mean it in the sense of militarising men. That is happening in our educational world at this moment, and it is forsaking all our history.[10]

This outburst and others of a similar nature were largely made in response to the growing number of military cadet schemes. Yet these very same schemes were largely responsible for keeping youngsters within the framework of the law and instilling them with a sense of self-discipline. Furthermore, since nobody could accurately predict the duration of the war it made perfect sense to prepare the nation's youth for the prospect of military service. This process did not indicate an abandonment of historical traditions, it was simply a sensible response to an ongoing crisis. In the event, and mainly because the majority of MPs argued that democracy equated with giving the general public a choice, public schools were retained and youth groups continued to flourish.

In terms of the children's future and the general post-war educational system however, science versus religion debates continued to dominate political discussions. Eventually a compromise was reached and there was a clear consensus that, even aside from religious concerns, schools needed to teach more science, particularly to city children who were more likely to be involved in manufacturing and industrial pursuits. As one MP proclaimed with enthusiasm: 'Science is going to control the future of nations. The nation will be on top which is best scientifically equipped. From that point of view alone our children should be scientifically minded in future to a degree which it was not possible for earlier generations to attain.'[11]

Nevertheless, the recognition that science was an important component of the school curriculum did not mean the exclusion of religion. Convincing arguments were put forward for the inclusion of religious instruction as a compulsory subject. Fears of a Germanic-style education system with its abhorrent potential consequences loomed large within these arguments; but there was also an overriding view that, as a faith-based nation, Christian principles were fundamental to British society. Since Britain was a caring democracy that was involved in fighting totalitarianism in order to protect such principles.

Christianity and scientific endeavour, therefore, needed to coexist within the British education system. The Christian children's author Clive Staples Lewis tried to explain this need in simple terms on BBC radio:

What they do [scientists] when they want to explain the atom, or something of that sort, is to give you a description out of which you make a mental picture. But then they warn you that this picture is not what scientists actually believe. What the scientists believe is a mathematical formula. The pictures are only there to help you understand the formula. They are not really true in the way the formula is; they do not give you the real thing but only something more or less like it. They are only meant to help, and if they do not help you can drop them. The thing itself cannot be pictured it can only be expressed mathematically. We are in the same boat here. We believe that the death of Christ is just that point in history at which something unimaginable from outside shows through into our own world. And if we cannot picture even the atoms of which our own world is built, of course we are not going to be able to picture this. Indeed, if we found that we could fully understand it, that very fact would show it was not what it professes to be – the inconceivable, the uncreated, the thing from beyond nature, striking down into nature like lightening. You may ask what good it will be to us if we do not understand it. But that is easily answered. A man can eat his dinner without understanding exactly how food nourishes him. A man can accept what Christ has done without knowing how it works: indeed, he certainly would not know how it works until he has accepted it. We are told that Christ was killed for us, that his death washed out our sins, and that by dying He disabled death itself. That is the formula. That is Christianity. That is what has to be believed.[12]

C.S. Lewis, who later went on to write allegorical children's series *The Chronicles of Narnia*, was employed by the BBC to impart his views about faith throughout the war. His talks were uplifting and reassuring in the dark days of the Blitz, they were also littered with witticisms and spiritual encouragement. He constantly reminded his listeners of 'How monotonously alike all the great tyrants and conquerors have been: how gloriously different the Saints.'[13]

Rhetoric aside, for the architect of the 1944 Education Act, R.A. Butler, there were more practical considerations to address before faith schools could be fully incorporated into a state education system. Prior to the war there were a total of 797 schools with defective premises; 211 of them had been placed on a Board of Education blacklist. The worst of these school buildings were to be found in Cumberland, Durham and Devon, but, courtesy of the Luftwaffe, city schools in particular were now in dire straits. Many needed to be totally rebuilt, and others needed to be shored up and supplemented by prefabricated huts.

Butler was also required to negotiate teacher training programmes with the leaders of various Christian denominations. This was a challenging and tortuous task, since hitherto Roman Catholic nuns were instructed on teaching methods by Roman Catholic priests, and worked in Catholic schools as unpaid teachers. The Church of England also had its own teacher training colleges. Under the terms of the new act however, all teachers were to be given a standard training and paid a standard salary.

Not surprisingly, these terms were unpopular with some religious organisations, since they would be required to pay out far more money in order to fund their staff at faith schools. Indeed, during the process of formulating the initial bill, Butler was forced to use all his powers of persuasion in an effort to bring religious leaders on board and gain their support. Writing in 1943, he did assure religious leaders of his intention to include faith education in the school curriculum:

Dear Mitcheson,

Thank you for letting me have a copy of Father Bean's letter and the petition signed by members of the Anglican Church of St Michael and of the Roman Catholic Church of Our Lady of Hal, Camden Town. I should like your constituents to know that it is the Government's intention that religious teaching shall have a definite and assured place in the school day and that all our children shall be given the opportunity of being brought up in the faith of their parents. I fully recognise that the rights of conscience must be inviolate and that we must work out arrangements whereby children receive distinctive denominational religious teaching if their parents so desire. It follows from this that I fully recognise that denominational schools have a continuing part to play in our educational system. I have been devoting my attention for two years now to devising ways of assisting them to play their part in the educational advance for which the time is now ripe. Further help can, however, only come from a public purse and my task is to frame a plan which judged in its denominational and secular aspects, will be accepted by the public at large.

Yours Sincerely
R.A. Butler[14]

Butler had already confirmed this stance when, earlier in the war, he applauded schoolchildren for their part in the war effort:

The schools and scholars have been brought more into the life of the nation through the share which they taken and are taking in our war effort. Children are doing their bit by helping with salvage work, the collection of waste, school savings groups, digging for victory, making comforts for the troops and adopting ships. All this practical work and practical service is worth many a classroom lesson in citizenship. They offer the first beginning of teaching children to realise they have something to give to the common stock. Indeed, I believe that activities of this kind may well be ancillary to the religious education which we are anxious should have its rightful place in the life of schools, inasmuch as Christianity is not only a faith to be followed but a life to be lived.[15]

In fact, there is no indication that Butler ever considered the prospect of excluding religious education from his proposals for educational reform. His overriding problem centred on the need to incorporate all denominations equally, and in a way that would satisfy all concerned. Therefore, it is not surprising that an analysis of the correspondence that took place between Butler and Church leaders in the years 1940–44 reveals a level of exasperation on the part of the former. Juggling the needs and demands of various faith interests and distilling them into one major piece of legislation was challenging to say the least. During a time of such physical devastation it also seems remarkable to many that religious leaders and politicians paid genuine attention to safeguarding the souls of children. Arguably, it was this same genuine concern that engendered compassion for all children and not just those who were indigenous to Britain. A group of frequently overlooked city children were those who had fled Nazi Germany and Austria. As many of these as possible were housed in suitable billets in reception areas, but since their mothers were also homeless when they arrived in Britain they frequently remained in cities as family units. The gratitude of these mothers however, was unmistakable – as social worker Eileen Potter recorded in her diary:

> I have to be at Whitechapel to pick up a party of children. One mother comes up to me and asks me to keep an eye on her boy, as he is a refugee from Vienna, and cannot speak much English. Another elderly mother with a strong German accent comes to me and says how grateful she feels towards England. 'It is the best country for children.'[16]

Petitions from church members across the length and breadth of Britain continued to flutter onto Butler's desk at Whitehall imploring him to construct a faith-based educational framework for their children. Imbuing children with a strong faith was, they argued, the only possible armour against moral corruption. This strength of feeling from the British public towards the moral upbringing of their children was impossible to ignore. Thus *The Times* continued to support the new crusade and C.S. Lewis was asked to explain the concept of the Christian soul during a BBC broadcast for the Home Service:

> Unbelievers complain that Christianity's a very selfish religion. 'Isn't it very selfish, even morbid, they say, 'to be always bothering about the inside of your soul instead of thinking of humanity?' Now what would an N.C.O. say to a soldier who had a dirty rifle and when told to clean it replied, 'But sergeant, isn't it very selfish, even morbid, to be always bothering about the inside of your own rifle instead of thinking about the United Nations?' Well we needn't bother about what the N.C.O. would actually say. You see the point. The man is not going to be of much use to the United Nations if his rifle isn't fit to shoot quickly. In the same way,

people acting from themselves won't do much real permanent good to other people.

Let me explain that. History isn't just the story of bad people doing bad things. It's quite as much a story of people trying to do doing good things. But somehow, something goes wrong. Take the common expression 'cold as charity'. How did we come to say that? From experience. We've learned how unsympathetic and patronising and conceited charitable people often are. And yet hundreds and thousands of them started out really anxious to do good and when they'd done it; somehow it wasn't as good as it ought to have been. The old story: what you are comes out in what you do. A crab apple tree cannot produce eating apples. As long as the old self is there its taint will be all over we do. We try to be religious and become Pharisees. We try to be kind and become patronising. Social service ends in red tape of officialdom. Unselfishness becomes a form of showing off. I don't mean of course that we're to stop trying to be good. We've got to do the best we can. If the soul's fool enough to go into battle with a dirty rifle he mustn't run away. But I do mean that the real cure lies far deeper. Out of our self and into Christ we must go.[17]

By May 1944 Butler's Education Bill had passed successfully through the House of Commons and the House of Lords and became an act. Henceforth, Butler's Education Act was hailed as a much-needed modern and radical reform, though there were also those who felt that he should have gone much further in levelling social inequities. Essentially the legislation provided free education for all, raised the school-leaving age to 15 and divided schools into grammar, secondary modern and technical schools. Entry to grammar schools was based on the eleven-plus examination, which replaced the traditional scholarships. Thanks to overwhelming public support, the new moral crusaders also achieved their objectives, since within the 1944 act religious education was made compulsory for all schools. Collective Christian worship thus began for all school-aged children at the start of each day in school assembly halls across the country. In addition, churches from all denominations were able to keep control over their curriculum and obtain state funding to assist with the day-to-day running of their schools.[18]

Notes

1 Padley, R. and Cole M., *Report to the Fabian Society* (1940), pp. 236–7.
2 Oral history testimony: Williams, Iris, 2011.
3 Gardiner, J., *The Blitz: The British Under Attack* (2010), p. 263.
4 Information taken from Haslum, M and Haslum, D., *Filton Parish Church – a history and a guide.*
5 Gardiner, J., *The Blitz: The British Under Attack* (2010), p. 247.
6 'The Leader' in *The Times*, 13 February 1941.
7 'The New Crusade' in *Journal of Education*, 21 February 1941, vol. LXXVII, no. 1989, p. 137.
8 'Letters to the Editor' in *Journal of Education*, 14 March 1941, vol. LXXVII, no. 1982, p. 209.
9 Ibid.
10 Hansard House of Commons Parliamentary Debates, 5th Series, 16 June 1942, col. 1431.
11 Ibid.
12 Lewis, C.S., *Mere Christianity* – publication based on a series of lectures given in wartime for the BBC (1942), p. 55.
13 Ibid., p. xx.
14 Letter from President of the Board of Education R.A. Butler to Micheson, dated 17 June 1943.
15 R.A. Butler, address to local education authorities, teachers and youth organisations at Southpark High School Lincoln, 24 September 1941, *Journal of Education*, vol. LXXVIII, no. 2021.
16 Garfield, S., *We Are At War* (2005), p. 120.
17 Lewis, C.S., BBC radio lecture for the Home Service, *Beyond Personality – Mere Men*, broadcast 21 March 1944.
18 It is perhaps also worth noting that the numbers of pupils on waiting lists for places at faith schools in the United Kingdom still exceeds that of ordinary state schools.

14

The Legacy

O ne of the most astonishing features of British wartime history is the speed and determination with which the nation's politicians chose to initiate and implement social reform. An analysis of parliamentary debates for the period reveals an unprecedented level of political good will and altruism in this respect, and a genuine cross-party consensus on a number of key issues that affected children. Such sentiments as those expressed by Sir Ernest Shepperson were commonplace within the corridors of power:

> I have a daughter who was at school, apparently very healthy. She went from school to Newnham College, Cambridge, where she had measles and later developed a cough. At Cambridge she was X rayed. T.B. was indicated. Immediately she was sent to the T.B. hospital and colony at Papworth. She has now, after some nine months, returned home practically cured; my wife and I say, and say very sincerely. 'Thank God for Papworth.' What Papworth has done for my daughter I want to be available for everybody's daughters. I do not desire to see 'possibilities' which will enable by daughter to be cured without similar possibilities being available for my fellow man.[1]

When it came to the issue of child welfare there was no hint of cynicism within Whitehall. Everyone, in all political parties, agreed that children needed to be a priority and, certainly by 1944, the government had done much to improve the health and welfare of British children. Free school meals and milk had become the norm, there was free orange and blackcurrant juice available for babies and widespread nursery provision for the under-5s. Successful vaccination programmes and health education campaigns had brought many childhood epidemics under control and, with the inclusion of religious education in the 1944 Education Act, their spiritual welfare was also in hand. In view of this admirable record in the field of childcare, ministers could be perhaps be forgiven for being in self-congratulatory mood. Therefore, it was with considerable disquiet and shock that they discovered that many children were living in destitute conditions; homeless, repressed, beaten and abused. A student social worker named Phyllis Noble, working in a Family Welfare Association office in Deptford, recorded a visit to a poor Irish family living in a nearby slum:

> To think that such squalor can still exist! I can never forget that smoke filled room, the mouldy cabbage in the corner, the bowl with the dirty water on the bare boards, the toddler wandering about in his threadbare shirt and no shoes. Nor the horror I felt when Mr Doyle said in his heavy Irish accent, but so casually, 'There's another behind you' – and I turned and saw a pile of rags on the bare springs of the bed, and hidden in the rags a dirty, tiny baby.[2]

The first indications that all was not well in the world of children were revealed in surveys conducted by middle-class women's groups. 'Our Towns: A Close Up' was published by these groups in 1943 and revealed a level of child poverty, neglect and abuse that was astounding. Indeed, their findings were later used as evidence for the need for a family allowance to be paid directly to mothers, and the need for child protection reform. The surveys highlighted the fact that both city and country children were suffering in large numbers, and while the former were more visible, the latter were equally neglected and abused.

Then, on 15 July 1944, *The Times* published a letter, written by Labour Peer Lady Marjory Allen, with regard to child welfare that prompted an extraordinary public reaction. In fact, no other single issue throughout the war produced as much correspondence to the editor. Lady Allen, like the Conservative MP Lady Astor before her, had agitated for child welfare reform. But it was not until the publication of her strongly worded letter, which outlined the incidents of child cruelty and neglect, alongside the stringent and sometimes sadistic conditions of local authority children's homes, that politicians began to sit up and take notice. Such children collectively became known as 'children deprived of a normal home life' or 'nobody's children'. Lady Allen wrote: 'Many thousands of these children are being brought up under repressive conditions. The social upheaval caused by the war has not only increased this army of unhappy children, but presents the opportunity for transforming their conditions.'[3]

The Times was consequently inundated with letters from the general public. It seemed as though everyone knew of a child who was being neglected, abandoned or badly treated. Gradually, politicians came to the realisation that despite their best efforts to improve the lives of children, something, somewhere, had gone horribly wrong. Convictions for serious offences against children in England and Wales before the war amounted to 800. This number had risen in the last year of the war to 1,700. Furthermore, prosecutions were only brought in front of the magistrates in extreme cases. It was estimated that voluntary bodies working to prevent cruelty to children actually dealt with far in excess of 100,000 cases a year.[4]

By 1944 over 2,000 children were in local authority homes. Many of them had been orphaned in the Blitz, some of them simply abandoned by their parents, and others had no homes to go to. The plight of these children, and others who roamed the streets surviving on their wits and little else, were a pitiful legacy. Incidents of burglary increased, but it was usually items of food that were stolen as homeless juveniles scrabbled about trying to stave off their hunger pangs. This shameful situation was compounded in January 1945 when a young boy (aged 13) named Dennis O'Neil was beaten to death by his foster father on a farm in North Wales. He suffered a heart attack due to prolonged malnutrition and severe beatings. He had septic blisters all over his body and weighed less than 4 stone. As the details of this dreadful tragedy were reported in the press the nation reeled in shock. Subsequently, details of other extreme cases of cruelty rose to the surface, until the full and horrific level of wartime child abuse was finally exposed. In response to these revelations of atrocities towards children Lady Allen produced a poignant leaflet entitled 'Whose Children', which was given nationwide press coverage. Home Secretary Herbert Morrison established two public enquiries in an effort to discover the facts behind what had now become a national scandal.

The Curtis Committee was entreated with the task of uncovering the facts about child welfare in England and Wales, and the Clyde Committee did likewise in Scotland. Their subsequent reports contained a catalogue of wartime child abuse that further shocked the nation. Although it is worth remembering that, just as notions of childhood differed somewhat in the 1940s from present day interpretations, so too did the definition of abuse. Corporal punishment at school and at home was viewed as a commonplace and accepted form of disciplining children. A father coming home from work and beating his son with a belt for an earlier misdemeanour was considered as quite normal behaviour. Similarly, teachers frequently administered beatings with a cane to schoolchildren for forgetting their homework or disrupting a classroom was common. But the scale and level of ill-treatment uncovered by the Curtis and Clyde Committees went far beyond this everyday abuse. However, it should be noted that the percentage of abused children was still a minority, in terms of the whole population it was estimated that 10–15 per cent of children were ill-treated. Many cases of abuse were never reported however, and it is likely that this figure was closer to 20 per cent.[5]

The majority of British children in 1945 were normal thriving youngsters, who despite the circumstances of war remained curious, adventurous, playful and contented. Moreover they greeted Victory in Europe Day with enthusiasm and euphoria, as Iris Williams from Bristol recalled: 'There were no muffled bells on that day I can tell you, the church bells rang out across the country. It was such a joyous day. Finally, our men would be coming home and we would all be able to live normal lives again. It was a wonderful celebration.'[6]

Most children were petted and spoiled with numerous treats on VE Day. There were street parties, fireworks and bonfires, concerts, dancing and puppet shows as manifestations of gaiety and merriment spread across the country. Victory celebrations were a life-affirming mixture of joy, wonder and relief.

However, the issue of child ill-treatment could not be swept under the carpet, and amid the joyous celebrations the children who had paid such a cost for victory were not forgotten, either by politicians or members of the general public. Thus, as the victory bells rang out from churches to celebrate a well-deserved victory for Britain and her allies, and Churchill proclaimed in his victory speech that 'the evil doers now lie prostrate before us', there were many across the country who realised with dismay that although the hard-fought war against the evils of Nazism had been won, another persistent and sinister evil remained on their own doorstep. As Lord Strabolgi later stated:

I suggest that it is a very disturbing fact. There remain callous, incompetent or grossly cruel parents and guardians which, according to statistics, do not diminish in number ... A great deal of work is done by voluntary bodies by way of warning, admonishing, advising, and in many cases they take it upon themselves to report grave cases to the police which it is their duty as citizens to do. Very often these warnings and persuasions are effective up to a point. But there are many other cases where the children continue to suffer and where the neighbours are too timid or indifferent to take action. Therefore, the extent of evil is very great indeed.[7]

While much of the problem stemmed from the child evacuation schemes, this was not the whole story. In fact, although children were less visible in the countryside, especially those who were billeted on isolated farms, city children were just as liable to be victims of mistreatment. There were children who were evacuated who found far better homes in the reception areas than those they had left behind, but also children who had found themselves in dire circumstances with no one to turn to for help. Some of the children who had stayed with their parents in the cities had also suffered appalling treatment. It seemed as though even the basic protection of children had been disregarded on a grand scale.

The Curtis and Clyde Reports laid the blame for the horrendous treatment of children firmly at the doors of both central and local government. Poor and inadequate record keeping, inefficient filing of notes and inspector's reports, overlooked warning signs, unheeded phone calls and incompetent staff had all contributed to the tragic catalogue of child abuse. Divided responsibilities within official departments with the left hand not knowing what the right hand was doing had generated serious oversights in the administration of child welfare. This problem, combined with a general apathy towards the care of children, lay at the crux of child neglect. For many within the House of Commons and the House of Lords, the reports merely confirmed what most had already suspected; namely that things had gone dangerously awry in the field of child protection. Reform was therefore not only necessary, but urgently demanded. Conservative MP for Farnham, Mr Nicholson, was amongst those emotive voices who called for change. His views were published in the *Guardian*:

He could scarcely believe that the government was unaware of the deep sense of disquiet felt by every section of the population as a result of the Curtis Report … A melancholy and ugly picture had been presented and the whole volume was a sorry condemnation of the inspection system and of the Ministry of Health which had received the inspector's reports and had done nothing about them.[8]

In many respects however, the official reports highlighted the tendency of local authorities to ignore central government directives. Therefore, even when child protection policies were initiated in Whitehall they were often not implemented as intended. Clearly, central government needed to take a firmer stance in the field of child protection. With this in mind, the government drew up new legislation that placed the Home Office at the centre for all child welfare. This legislation was introduced with a sense of urgency and became the Children's Act in July 1948. It has since been recognised as 'the most comprehensive and humane children's legislation in history'.[9]

The act amounted to a complete turnaround in government policy. Hitherto, local authorities had assumed responsibility for children in their areas. Whereas the new legislation shifted emphasis and responsibility back towards central government. The appointment of the Home Office as overseer of newly established children's committees within local authorities was an attempt to fortify the new act with a strong political backbone. The fact that local authorities were not even allowed to design their own childcare committees under the act, nor were they able to appoint their own children's officers without the approval of the Secretary of State, emphasised this move towards central control. The legislation also indicated in no uncertain terms that government ministers held local authorities responsible for the dereliction of child protection duties and the subsequent tragedies that had befallen children.

Henceforth, all children's officers were required to undergo training, and they became the foundation of the new childcare and protection legislation. The system of fostering children with suitably vetted and approved foster parents was widely extended, and the number of residential care homes was reduced in size and number. All of this new legislation was designed to prevent future child abuse as the MP for north Bradford explained: 'The object of this central authority is to make sure that never again shall a child die of cruelty and neglect such as Dennis O'Neil, and that never again shall a child suffer from the confusion and muddle in administration.'[10]

There were many magistrates, teachers, social workers and parents who suggested that the new act was a case of shutting the stable door after the horse had bolted. Furthermore, the act failed to protect the most vulnerable group of children. These were the orphans, or in some cases assumed orphans, who were sent out to the British colonies in the post-war years. Many of these children were also shipped out to far-flung corners of the empire courtesy of Church organisations, including the Church of England, the Roman Catholic Church and the Methodist Church. The newly formed Children's Act did not cover policies of forced migration. Nevertheless, the legislation did amount to a major revolution in childcare approaches. The importance of family units was stressed and social workers and children's officers spent more time shoring up mother–child bonds. Their efforts were supported by psychologists, psychiatrists and distinguished paediatricians such as James Spence. Indeed, his speech entitled 'The Purpose of the Family' was extremely influential and ranked alongside the works of Anna Freud and John Bowlby in terms of dictating the subsequent course of childcare policy.

Wartime research findings of such professionals had also generated renewed interest in child development and a national cross-cultural survey into child health was initiated; one that included over 5,000 children who had been born in March 1946. Not surprisingly, the survey concluded that women who were married to unskilled labourers struggled the most to make ends meet, feed their children and organise their daily lives to incorporate necessary housework, shopping and visits to the baby clinics. By the time their children had reached the age of 2 they were nearly an inch shorter than children growing up in professional middle-class families. Working-class mothers were often in poor health because, on a meagre budget, they often gave only their children food and went without sustenance themselves. Such women could frequently be found in large numbers waiting outside the factory gates, near the dockyards or building sites on Friday evenings to collect the wage packets of their husbands.

Ostensibly, these mass gatherings represented an attempt by many wives and mothers to get their hands on the wages before the money was spent by their husbands in public houses or betting shops, and it was scenes such as these that had ensured the introduction of the Family Allowance Act. Subsequently, even women whose husbands squandered their wages were able to spend some money directly on their children.

Payment of family allowances also enabled some mothers to return to the home when they would otherwise have been required, from necessity, to continue working. In terms of endorsing the advice of childcare experts, women's magazines stayed on message, reporting childcare issues and encouraging mothers to return to the hearth and home on a weekly basis. The art of motherhood was extolled and elevated, healthy mother and child bonds were claimed to be the cure for all social ills. From a government standpoint this was a difficult message to wholeheartedly convey. On the one hand, ministers were eager to follow the advice of child guidance experts, but on the other hand, the acute post-war labour shortage had prompted the new prime minister, Clement Atlee, to ask women to continue working, even if only part-time, until a solution to the shortages could be found. Eventually, politicians embarked on a massive immigration policy to resolve the labour shortages, and they began to close down nurseries in an attempt to drive women back into the home. In truth, many married women with children were relieved by such a policy, since they were struggling to cope with the demands of home and work. Some, however, continued to work despite these demands.

Judy Fryd, for instance, had married in 1936 and had four children, the first of whom had serious learning difficulties. Fryd encountered such problems and prejudice that she was instrumental in founding the Association of Parents of Backward Children. The association is now known as the Royal Society for Mentally Handicapped Children and Adults (MENCAP). 'My career was always going to be in politics,' she once remarked, 'I just didn't realise that it was the mentally handicapped corner I would be fighting.'[11]

For Judy and women like her, the post-war years would be spent campaigning for a better understanding and acceptance of children with challenging mental, emotional and physical problems. There was also a move to include some children with disabilities and medical conditions such as epilepsy into mainstream schools for the first time. Undoubtedly, many of these societal changes were implemented as a result of wartime observations and experience. Child guidance clinics, child psychologists and the Children's Act had fundamentally altered the way adults viewed the needs of children. But some societal changes were so subtle they were difficult to discern. From 1939 onwards the upbringing of a large number of children had effectively been handed over to teachers, and the education system began to assume more and more responsibility for certain aspects of child rearing.

By the end of the war thousands of normal child–parent relationships had been ruptured, many beyond repair. Some parents had been totally deprived of the joys of the parenting experience, whilst many children had been subjected to inadequate or detrimental parental role models. These same children were later unable to develop the crucial parenting skills they needed to pass on to the next generation. Therefore, it can be argued that in some respects, a cycle of child abuse was created during the war from which Britain has never fully recovered. Since, as social workers and children's officers observed, the pattern is rarely broken. Consequently, many children were brought up in the post-war years by insecure parents with unrealistic expectations of the education system: 'They, their children and their children's children become the abused and abusers of the future – tomorrow, and tomorrow and tomorrow.'[12]

But the work of children's officers, teachers, child guidance experts and paediatricians in the post-war years did involve breaking such patterns, and in many cases they were successful. Indeed, the mere recognition that patterns of abuse were repetitive was a revelation, and one that was underpinned by wartime research. As Anna Freud had observed, even children with abusive parents still loved those parents. Therefore, the most powerful and lasting legacy of city children growing up during the Blitz had been to highlight the strength and significance in terms of overall child development, of emotional ties. In particular, they had revealed the importance of mother–child bonds and family units. In doing so, they had revolutionised approaches to childcare. Furthermore, the large numbers of distressed evacuees confirmed the detrimental effects of child–parent separation and detachment. Armed with this crucial knowledge, children's officers were subsequently able to help thousands of children and their parents.

Once the long-awaited National Health Service was established, the lives of most children continued to improve. Free glasses, free dental care, free medical inspections and medical screening, free doctor's appointments, school nurses, educational psychologists, orthopaedic spinal clinics to improve posture and foot clinics to correct flat feet, along with comprehensive vaccination and health education programmes all combined to improve and monitor a child's health and development.

However, in addition to the revolutionary 1948 Children's Act, blitzed children left another enduring legacy, and one which has been frequently overlooked by scholars who have documented children's history – namely that of the adventure playground movement. Alongside her efforts to gain homes and care for 'nobody's children', Lady Allen was at the forefront of the adventure playground concept. Many teachers, parents and social workers had noted that children in blitzed cities were never happier than when they were grubbing around in dirt and rubble, playing in old burnt out vehicles, constructing imaginary dens and bases in bombed-out buildings or making swings and slides from bits of rope and wood. It may have seemed incomprehensible to most adults, but children loved playing on bombsites. Existing playgrounds, Lady Allen argued, were too sanitised and left little room for a child's imagination, nor for a child to be challenged and use their own initiative. Children were happier swinging on old rubber tyres, tackling obstacle courses, battling with ropes and constructing dens from old bricks, digging in the mud and play-fighting with sticks. Thus it transpired that besides the all-important official legislations, social reforms, the emergence of child guidance clinics and children's officers, children of the Blitz were singularly responsible for the birth of the adventure playground in Britain. A timely reminder for adults perhaps, that the majority of children of all ages and backgrounds, even when confronted by war, approached life as a big adventure.

Notes

1   Hansard House of Commons Parliamentary Debates, 5th Series, 30 June 1942, report to the Supply Committee, Sir Ernest Shepperson addressing the Minister of Health.
2   Kynaston, D., *A World to Build* (2007), p. 283.
3   Lady Allen, 'Editors Letters' in *The Times*, 15 July 1944.
4   Hansard House of Commons Parliamentary Debates, 25 March 1952, vol. 175, col. 924–60.
5   It should be noted that incidents of sexual abuse, in particular, often went unnoticed and unreported. Some war children only began to reveal their stories for the first time in 1998 and 1999, and most victims of such abuse

claimed that they had never told a soul about their suffering because they feared they would not be believed.

6   Oral history testimony: Williams, Iris, May 2011.

7   Hansard House of Commons Parliamentary Debates, 25 March 1952, vol. 175, col. 924–960.

8   The *Guardian*, 20 November 1946, p. 6.

9   *The Times*, 28 July 2008.

10   Hansard House of Commons Parliamentary Debates, 5th Series, 7 May 1948, col. 1647.

11   Kynaston, D., *A World to Build* (2007), p. 101.

12   Turner, J., *Behind Closed Doors* (1988), p. 74.

Bibliography

Brown, M. and Harris, C., *The Wartime House: Home Life in Wartime Britain 1939–1945* (2001).

Brown, M., *Put That Light Out: Britain's Civil Defence Services at War 1939–1945* (1999).

Cannadine, D., *Class in Britain* (1998).

Freud, A., *War and Children* (1943).

Gardiner, J., *The Blitz: The British Under Attack* (2010).

Garfield, S., *We Are At War: Diaries of Five Ordinary People in Extraordinary Times* (2005).

Hickman, T., *What Did You Do in the War Auntie? The BBC at War 1939–1945* (1995).

Kynaston, D., *A World to Build* (2007).

Lewis, C.S., *Mere Christianity* (1944).

Lowe, R., *The Welfare State in Britain Since 1945* (1993).

Packham, J., *Aspects of Social Policy the Child's Generation: Childcare Policy from Curtis to Houghton* (1975).

Padley, R. and Cole, M., *A Report to the Fabian Society* (1940).

Patten, M., *OBE Victory Cook Book* (1995).

Titmuss, R., *Problems of Social Policy* (1950).

Women's Group on Public Welfare, 'Our Towns: A Close Up' (1943).

Index